CAMBRIDGE
UNIVERSITY PRESS

CB081771

Cambridge Lower Secondary

Science

WORKBOOK 8

Mary Jones, Diane Fellowes-Freeman & Michael Smyth

CAMBRIDGE
UNIVERSITY PRESS

Shaftesbury Road, Cambridge CB2 8EA, United Kingdom

One Liberty Plaza, 20th Floor, New York, NY 10006, USA

477 Williamstown Road, Port Melbourne, VIC 3207, Australia

314–321, 3rd Floor, Plot 3, Splendor Forum, Jasola District Centre, New Delhi – 110025, India

103 Penang Road, #05–06/07, Visioncrest Commercial, Singapore 238467

Cambridge University Press & Assessment is part of the University of Cambridge.

It furthers the University's mission by disseminating knowledge in the pursuit of education, learning and research at the highest international levels of excellence.

www.cambridge.org
Information on this title: www.cambridge.org/9781108742856

First published 2012
Second edition 2021

20 19 18 17 16 15 14 13 12

Printed in Italy by L.E.G.O. S.p.A.

A catalogue record for this publication is available from the British Library

ISBN 978-1-108-74285-6 Paperback with Digital Access (1 year)

Additional resources for this publication at www.cambridge.org/delange

The exercises in this Workbook have been written to cover the Biology, Chemistry, Physics, Earth and Space and any appropriate Thinking and Working Scientifically learning objectives from the Cambridge Lower Secondary Science curriculum framework (0893). Some Thinking and Working Scientifically learning objectives and the Science in Context learning objectives have not been covered in this Workbook.

Contents

How to use this book

This workbook provides questions for you to practise what you have learned in class. There is a topic to match each topic in your Learner's Book. Each topic contains the following sections:

Focus: these questions help you to master the basics

Focus

In this exercise, you will decide what you can work out from a distance/time graph.

1 Which of these can be worked out from a distance/time graph?

Tick (✓) **one** box.

The force on an object. ☐
The speed of an object. ☐
The mass of an object. ☐
The weight of an object. ☐

2 Look at the distance/time graph for a train.

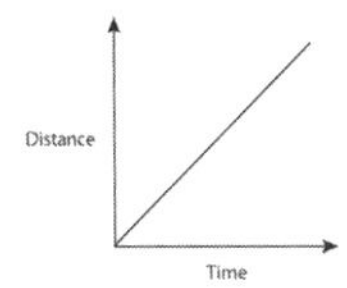

a Which of these distance/time graphs shows the train going faster?

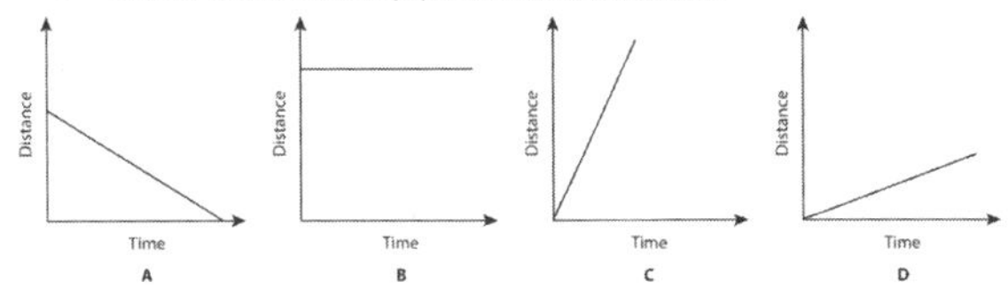

Write the letter. ....

b Which distance/time graph in part **a** shows **no** change in distance with time?

Write the letter. ....

Practice: these questions help you to become more confident in using what you have learnt

Practice

This exercise will give you practice in explaining the use of soil cores.

1 The core of peat has been removed from a bog. Scientists will study the pollen found in the core.

The end nearer to the left of the picture is from the top of the bog.

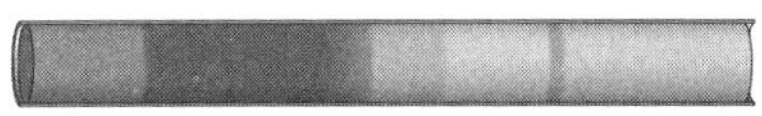

a Is the oldest peat from the top or the bottom of the bog?

....

b Why has the plant material, including pollen, not rotted in the peat bog?

....

....

c What are the scientists hoping to find out by studying the pollen found in the core?

Challenge: these questions will make you think very hard

Challenge

In this exercise, you will consider the variables that affect pressure in solids.

1 The picture shows part of the stem of a plant called a rose.

The stem has parts called thorns.

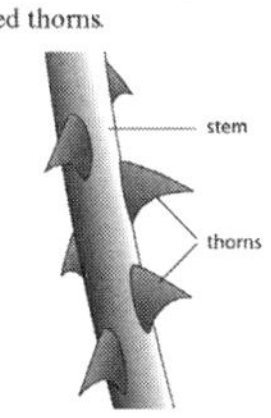

Explain why touching the thorns is more dangerous than touching other parts of the stem.

1 Respiration

> 1.1 The human respiratory system

Exercise 1.1 Structure and function in the respiratory system

This exercise helps you to recognise the parts of the respiratory system on a diagram. You can then try describing their functions, and think about what it would be like to travel down through the system.

Focus

The diagram shows the human respiratory system.

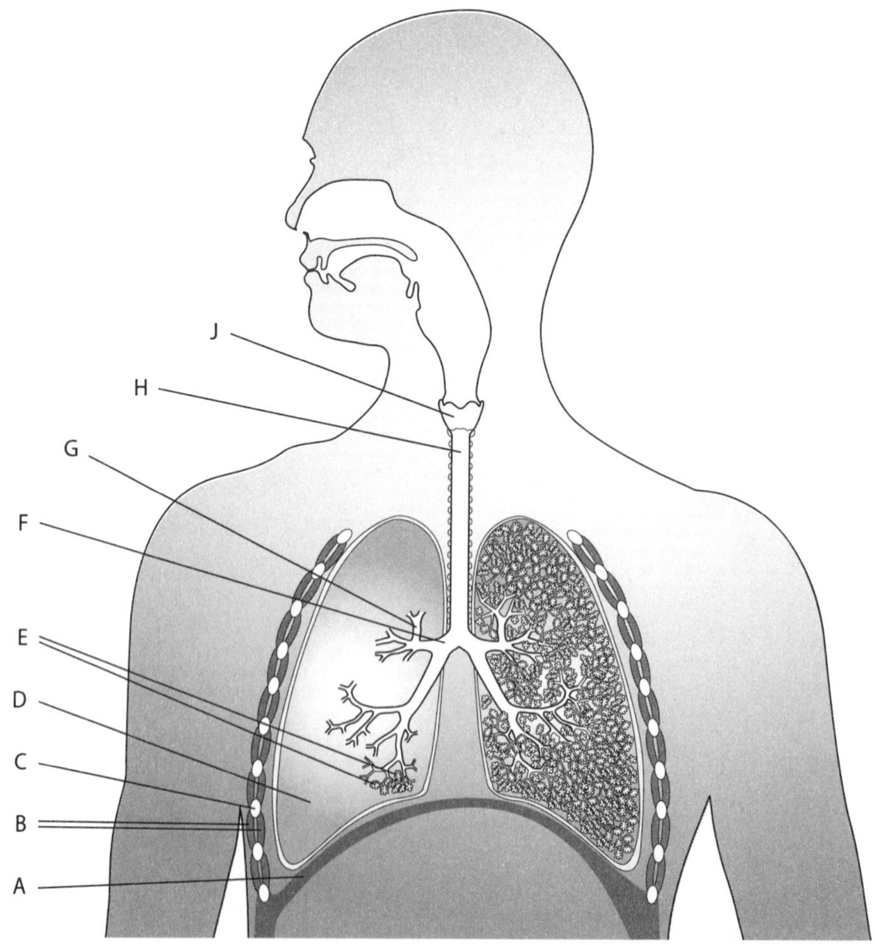

1 Complete the table by naming each of the parts shown on the diagram.

Choose from these names.

air sacs bronchiole bronchus diaphragm lung
larynx (voice box) intercostal muscles rib trachea

Letter	Name
A	
B	
C	
D	
E	
F	
G	
H	
J	

Practice

2 Describe the function of each of the labelled parts listed in this table.

Letter	Function
C	
D	
E	
F	
G	
H	
J	

Challenge

3 In your own words, describe the pathway that air takes as it travels from outside your body into the air sacs. If you like, you can make your description more interesting by writing as though you were a particle of oxygen.

› 1.2 Gas exchange

Exercise 1.2 Lung surface area and body mass

This exercise provides you with data about six different mammals. You will practise looking for correlations in data, and suggesting explanations for the patterns that you find.

Focus

The table shows the body masses of six mammals. It also shows the total surface area of the air sacs in the mammals' lungs.

Mammal	Body mass in g	Total surface area of air sacs in m^2
human	80 000	70
mouse	20	0.1
rabbit	1000	8
rat	300	0.8
sheep	68 000	60
fox	20 000	40

1 The entries in the table above are not in a very helpful order.

Complete the table below by reorganising the entries in a way that makes it easier to see any patterns in the data.

Mammal	Body mass in g	Total surface area of air sacs in m^2

Practice

2 Describe the relationship between body mass and total surface area of the air sacs.

....

....

Challenge

3 Suggest an explanation for the relationship you have described.

....

....

....

....

1.3 Breathing

Exercise 1.3A Measuring lung volumes

Focus

In this exercise, you complete a results table. Then you calculate mean values and draw a bar chart.

Sofia and Zara want to know if learners who play wind instruments in the school orchestra can push more air out of their lungs than learners who play stringed instruments.

The girls take a large, empty bottle. They mark a scale on the side to show volumes.

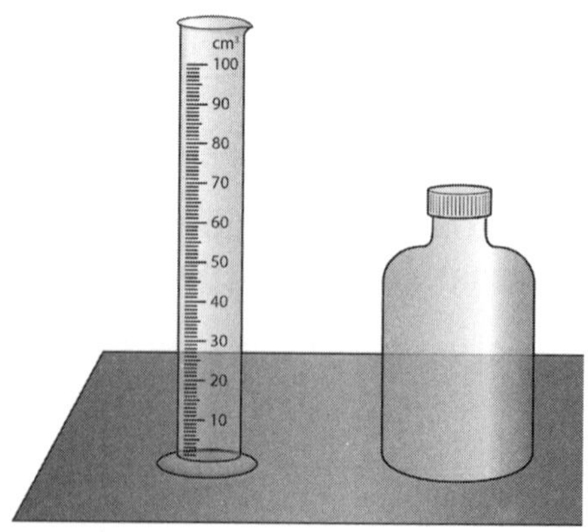

1 Describe how Sofia and Zara can make the scale on the bottle.

....

....

....

Sofia and Zara fill the bottle with water. They turn the full bottle upside down, with its open top in a large container of water.

Marcus plays a wind instrument. The girls ask Marcus to blow into the bottle as hard as he can. They use the scale to record how much water Marcus can push out of the bottle.

They then test eight more musicians.

Here are the results that Sofia and Zara collect.

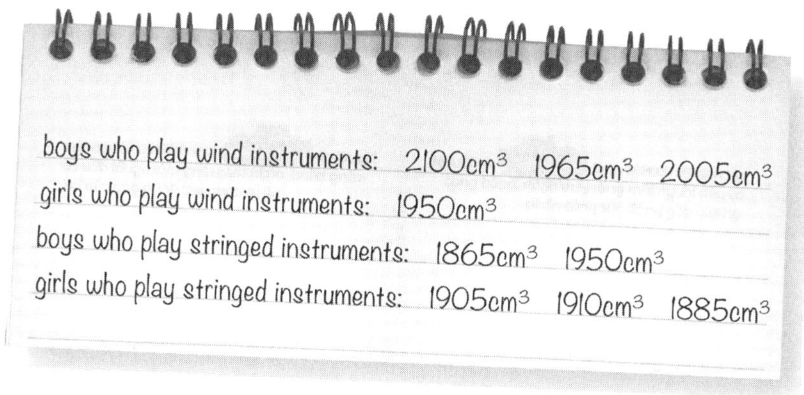

boys who play wind instruments: 2100cm^3 1965cm^3 2005cm^3
girls who play wind instruments: 1950cm^3
boys who play stringed instruments: 1865cm^3 1950cm^3
girls who play stringed instruments: 1905cm^3 1910cm^3 1885cm^3

2 Complete Sofia and Zara's results table.

Person	Boy or girl	Wind or string player	Volume displaced in cm^3
1	boy	wind	2100

3 Calculate the mean volume displaced (pushed out) for the boys who play wind instruments.

Remember: To calculate the mean of three values, add them up and divide by 3.

Show your working.

.... cm^3

4 Calculate the mean volume displaced for the boys who play stringed instruments.

Show your working.

.... cm^3

5 Calculate the mean volume displaced for the girls who play stringed instruments.

Show your working.

.... cm^3

6 Complete the bar chart to show Sofia and Zara's results.

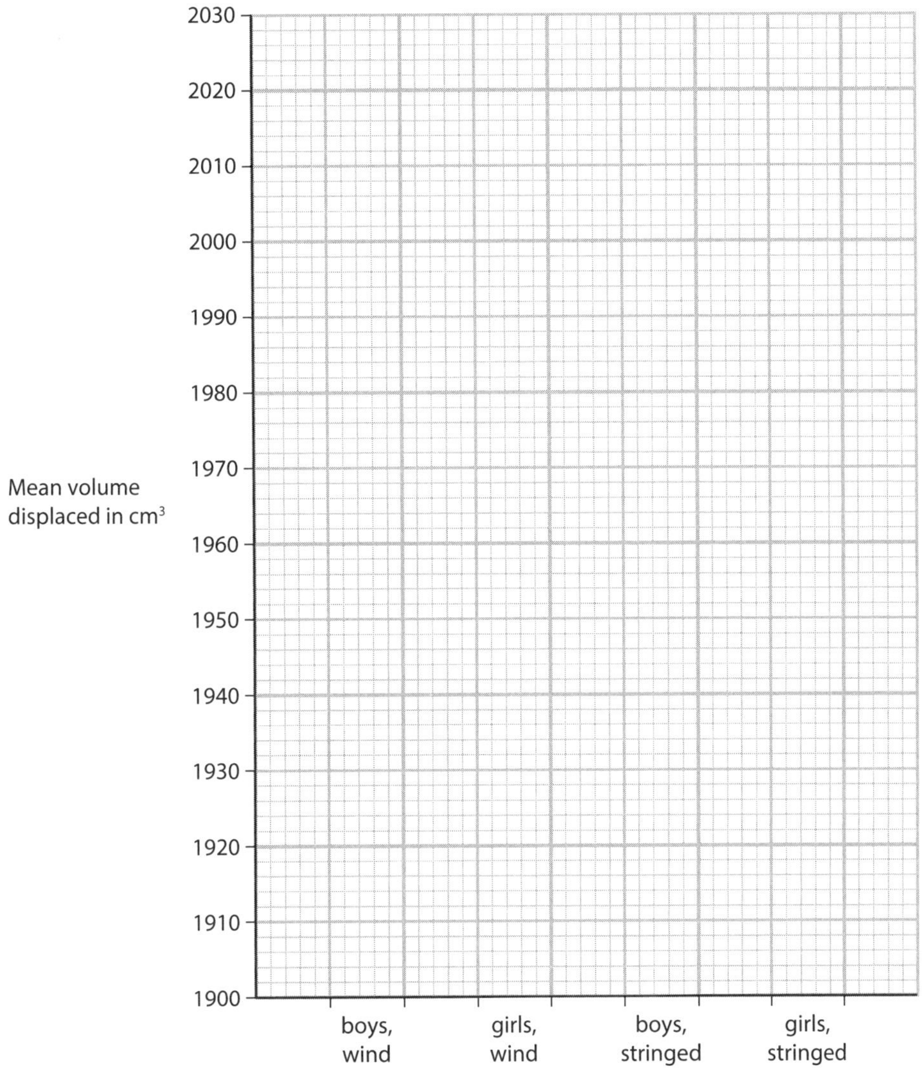

Exercise 1.3B Looking at data on lung volumes

Practice

In this exercise, you will look for patterns in data.

Then you think about how to improve an experiment.

Look at the experiment that Sofia and Zara did, which is described in Exercise 1.3A.

Sofia and Zara discuss what their results show.

1 Is Sofia right? Explain your answer.

....

....

....

....

2 Is Zara right? Explain your answer.

....

....

....

....

3 The girls' teacher says they cannot draw any definite conclusions from their results.

She asks them to try to improve their experiment.

What will improve the girls' experiment?

Tick (✓) **two** boxes.

Collecting more results from more people in the orchestra. ☐

Finding out whether playing a percussion instrument affects lung volume. ☐

Making three measurements for each person. ☐

Measuring how fast each person can run. ☐

Exercise 1.3C Lung volume at different ages

Challenge

In this task, you will practise finding information on a graph. You will do a simple calculation, and use evidence from the graph to make predictions.

Scientists measured the lung volumes of several hundred men and women of different ages. The people were asked to push out as much air from their lungs as they could, in one breath.

The mean values of the volume of air pushed out for each age group were calculated.

The graph shows the results.

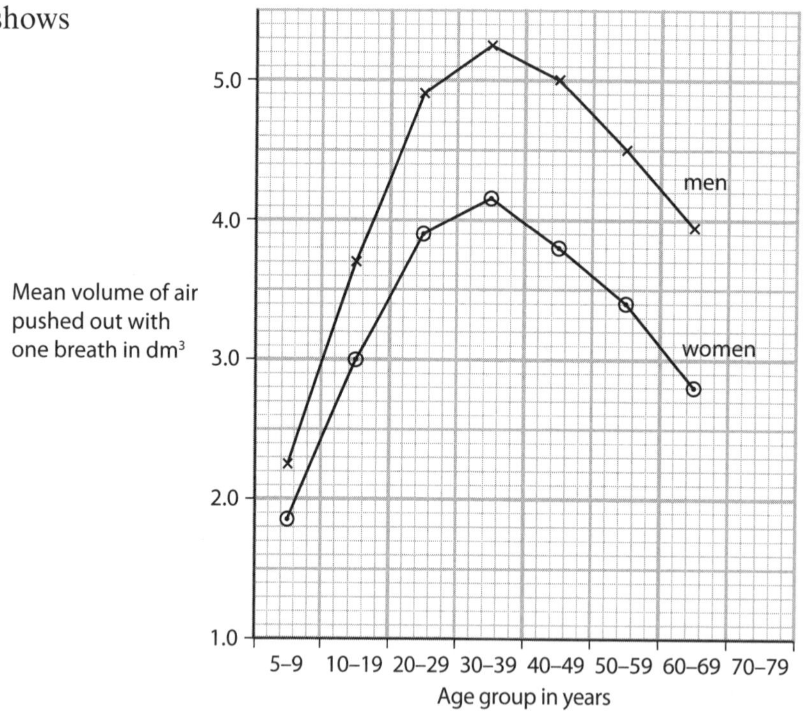

1 Suggest why the researchers collected results from several hundred men and women, rather than just a few in each age group.

....

....

....

2 State the mean volume of air pushed out for women in the 20–29 age group.

Remember to give the unit with your answer.

....

3 Calculate the difference between the mean volumes of air pushed out for men and women in the 40–49 age group.

Show your working.

....

4 Describe how the mean volume of air that can be pushed out by women changes with age.

....

....

....

....

5 Use the graph to predict a value for the mean volume of air that can be pushed out by men aged between 70 and 79.

....

1.4 Respiration

Exercise 1.4 Respiration by yeast

In this exercise, you will think about how to choose apparatus, and the correct way to use a thermometer. You make a prediction about temperature change and also think about using this apparatus to plan an experiment to test a hypothesis.

Focus

Yeast is a living microorganism. Sofia wants to find out what happens to the temperature of yeast when it respires.

She has some yeast mixed with water. She measures 25 cm^3 of the mixture and puts it into an insulated cup.

Then she adds 25 cm^3 of sugar solution.

1 One piece of apparatus that Sofia needs is missing from the diagram.

State what this apparatus is, and why Sofia needs it.

....

....

....

2 Sofia measures the temperature of the mixture of yeast and sugar solution in the cup.

How should Sofia measure the temperature?

Tick (✓) **all** the correct statements.

Make sure that her eyes are level with the meniscus in the thermometer to read the temperature. ☐

Stand the thermometer in the cup so it is resting on the bottom. ☐

Hold the thermometer in the liquid and stir gently. ☐

Make sure her eyes are level with the meniscus to read the temperature. ☐

Practice

3 Predict what will happen to the temperature of the mixture in the cup.

Explain your prediction.

Prediction ....

Explanation ....

....

4 Sofia has missed out something very important from her experiment.

What has she missed out?

Look at what Sofia is trying to find out.

Think about what she needs to do to be sure any temperature change she measures is due only to the yeast respiring.

....

....

....

Challenge

5 Describe how Sofia could use her apparatus to test this hypothesis:

> The more sugar the yeast is given, the faster it will respire.

....

....

....

....

....

....

....

1.5 Blood

Exercise 1.5A The components of blood

Focus

In this exercise, you will think about the three components that make up blood.

Human blood has three components:

- plasma
- red blood cells
- white blood cells.

1 Which of these three components is a liquid?

....

2 Which of these three components has nuclei?

....

3 Which component performs each of these functions?

a transporting oxygen from the lungs to all the respiring cells in the body

....

b protecting against pathogens that have got into the body

....

c transporting blood cells, nutrients and carbon dioxide

....

Exercise 1.5B Functions of blood components

Practice

In this exercise, you will think about suitable words to complete sentences about blood.

Choose the best words to complete the sentences.

antibodies **bacteria** **carbon dioxide** **cytoplasm**
glucose **haemoglobin** **least** **like** **nucleus**
most **oxygen** **plasma** **unlike**

Blood contains a pale yellow liquid, called ....

This liquid carries red blood cells and white blood cells around the body.

It also transports several different substances in solution, including

.... and ....

Red blood cells are the .... abundant cells in the blood.

Their function is to transport .... from the lungs to all the cells in the body that are respiring. To help them to do this, they contain a red pigment called ....

White blood cells, ... red blood cells, contain a nucleus.

Their function is to destroy pathogens, such as ...., that get into the body. Some of them do this by producing chemicals called ...., which attach themselves to the pathogens and kill them. Other white blood cells kill pathogens by taking them into their .... and digesting them.

Exercise 1.5C Rats at altitude

Challenge

In this challenging task, you will use information to make a prediction. You will draw a graph to display a set of results, and think about the design of an experiment.

Red blood cells carry oxygen around the body. At high altitudes, there is less oxygen in the air.

A team of scientists did an experiment to find out how the number of red blood cells in rats changed when the rats were taken to high altitude.

1 Make a prediction about what might happen to the number of red blood cells when the rats were taken to high altitude.

Explain your prediction.

....

....

....

....

....

....

This is what the scientists did.

- They kept one group of rats at sea level, and took another group to high altitude.
- They took blood samples from each rat on days 1, 3, 7, 15 and 20.
- They measured the number of red blood cells in a certain volume of blood from each rat. This is called the red blood cell count.
- They calculated the mean red blood cell count for each group of rats.

The table shows their results.

Time in days	Mean red blood cell count	
	Rats at sea level	Rats at high altitude
1	6.5	6.5
3	7.0	8.5
7	6.5	10.0
15	6.5	10.5
20	7.0	11.5

2 On the grid, construct line graphs to show these results.
Draw two lines on the same pair of axes.

Take care with the scale on the horizontal axis.

3 What was the independent variable in the experiment?

....

4 What was the dependent variable in the experiment?

....

5 Suggest **two** variables that the scientists should have kept the same.

....

....

6 Calculate the increase in red blood cell count for the rats at high altitude from day 1 to day 20.

Show your working.

....

7 Use your answer to question 6 to calculate the mean rate of increase per day.

Show your working.

....

8 After 20 days, the rats at high altitude were taken back down to sea level.

Predict what would happen to their red blood cell count over the next few weeks.

Explain your answer.

....

....

....

....

2 Properties of materials

2.1 Dissolving

Exercise 2.1A Using the correct scientific term

Focus

This exercise will help you to use the correct scientific terms.

Use the terms given below to label the diagrams. Each term may be used once, more than once or not at all.

dissolves	**solution**	**filtrate**	**solute**
mixture	**solvent**	**solid**	**volume**

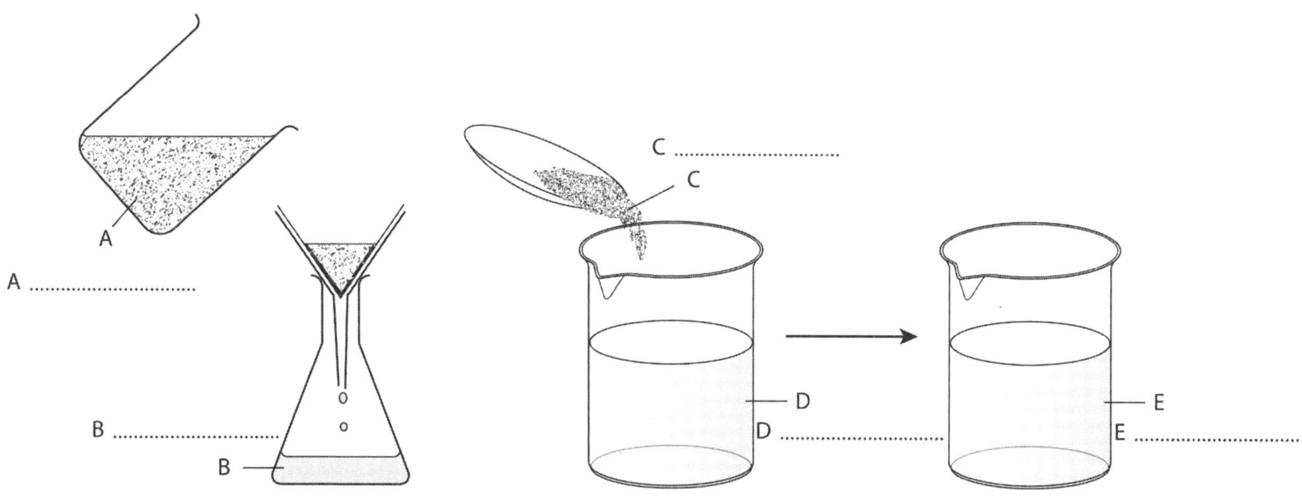

A ....

B ....

C ....

D ....

E ....

Exercise 2.1B What is the difference between these terms?

Practice

In this exercise, you will practise explaining the difference between terms.

1 Explain the difference between the terms transparent and opaque.

....

....

....

2 Explain the difference between the terms dissolving and melting.

....

....

....

3 Distinguish between the terms solute, solvent and solution.

....

....

....

....

....

Exercise 2.1C Explaining observations

Challenge

In this exercise, you will explain the reasons behind some observations.

When 20 g of salt is added to a beaker containing 100 g of water, the salt dissolves and seems to disappear as a solution is formed.

1 What is the mass now? ....

2 Explain your answer.

....

....

....

2.2 Solutions and solubility

Exercise 2.2A Using the correct scientific term

Focus

This exercise will help you to use the correct scientific terms.

Use the terms given below to complete the sentences. Each term may be used once, more than once or not at all.

concentrated	solubility	saturated solution
soluble	insoluble	diluted

1 A substance that will not dissolve in water is ....

2 Solutions A and B have the same volume of solvent, but solution A has more solute particles in it than solution B.

Solution A is more .... than solution B.

3 Sofia has added more and more copper sulfate to a beaker of water until no more will dissolve.

She has made a .... of copper sulfate.

4 Copper sulfate dissolves in water, so it is said to be

.... in water.

5 Marcus has added 50 cm^3 water to a solution of sodium chloride.

He has .... the solution.

Exercise 2.2B Looking at the solubility of three solutes

Practice

This exercise will help you to interpret results.

Zara, Arun and Marcus have investigated three solutes, A, B and C, to find out how soluble they are. They put water in their test tubes and measured how many spatulas of the solute they could add until no more would dissolve.

Zara has her test tubes ready, with the water added before she starts to add the solutes.

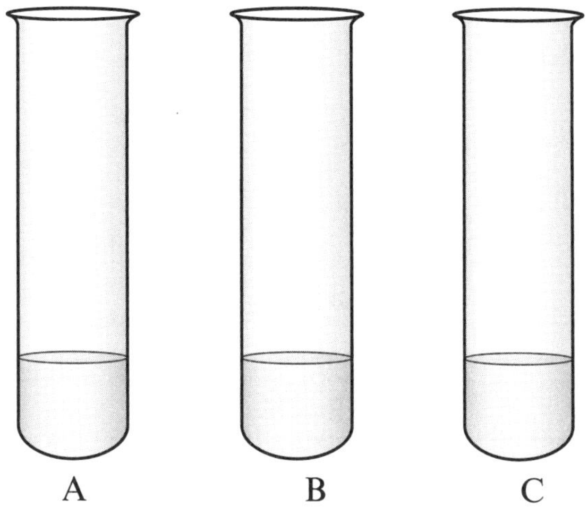

Marcus has his test tubes ready, with the water added before he starts to add the solutes.

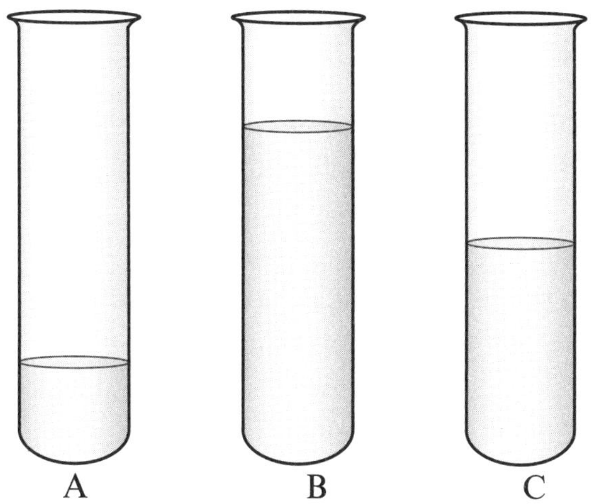

Arun has his test tubes ready, with the water added before he starts to add the solutes.

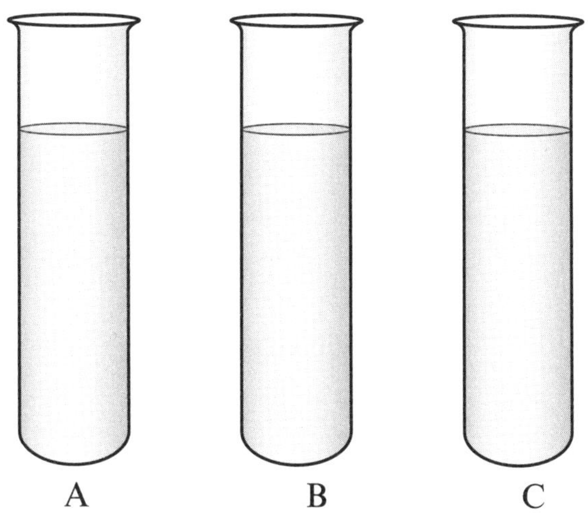

They each use the solutes in the same order and add them to their set of test tubes, working from left to right Here are their results.

Solute used	Number of spatulas of solute used until no more would dissolve		
	Zara	Marcus	Arun
A	3	3	9
B	1	3	3
C	2	3	6

1 Which solute did Zara find was the most soluble? ....

2 Which did she find the least soluble? ....

3 Look carefully at Arun's results. He has a different number of spatulas of solute added compared to Zara, but do Arun's results agree with Zara's findings? ....

4 Explain the difference in the reading that Zara and Arun got.

....

....

5 Marcus has the same number of spatulas for all three solutes. Explain why his results are so different from those of Zara and Arun.

....

....

....

....

....

....

Exercise 2.2C Making up a solution

Challenge

This exercise will help you to work out how to make solutions of the correct concentration.

Arun has a solution of copper sulfate labelled X.

1 Explain how he can make up a $100\,cm^3$ solution of copper sulfate that is:

a half as concentrated as solution X

....

....

b a quarter as concentrated as solution X

....

....

c half as concentrated as the solution in part **b**.

....

....

2 What steps can Arun take to ensure that his solutions are made up as accurately as possible?

....

....

2.3 Planning a solubility investigation

Exercise 2.3A Dissolving salt

Focus

In this exercise, you will interpret a graph and spot mistakes.

Marcus and Sofia are investigating how much salt they can dissolve in different volumes of water.

The volume of water they use is the independent variable.

This is what they do. Sofia measures out the volume of water. Marcus places the beaker of water on a top pan balance and adds salt, one spatula at a time, until no more dissolves. He measures the mass of salt added.

Here is their table of results.

Volume of water in cm^3	Mass of salt in g
10	4
20	9
30	13
40	16
50	20
60	26
70	26
80	30
90	32
100	36

Marcus plots this graph from their results.

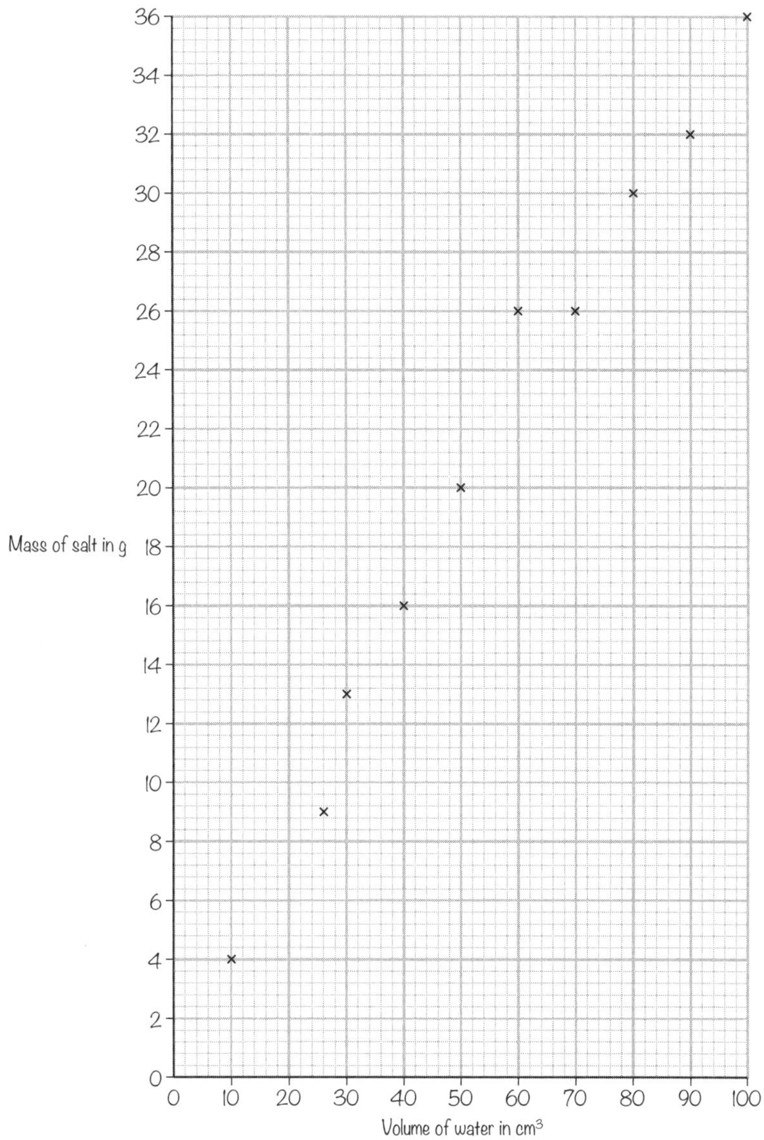

1 What was Sofia's prediction?

....

2 Which reading is plotted incorrectly? Draw a **red** circle around it on the graph.

3 Which other point does not fit the pattern of the graph? Draw a **blue** circle around this mass reading in the table, and around the point on the graph.

4 Draw a line of best fit.

5 Describe what the graph shows.

....

....

....

6 Was Sofia's prediction correct?

....

Exercise 2.3B Comparing the solubility of two salts: part 1

Practice

In this exercise, you will plan an investigation and interpret some results.

Arun and Marcus are asked to compare the solubility of two salts in water at room temperature. The two salts are labelled X and Y.

1 Name the independent variable in the investigation.

....

2 Name the dependent variable in the investigation.

....

3 List the control variables in the investigation.

....

....

4 Describe how Arun and Marcus will carry out this investigation. They have access to normal laboratory equipment. You may draw a diagram if this helps your description.

....

....

....

....

....

....

....

Exercise 2.3C Comparing the solubility of two salts: part 2

Challenge

Arun and Marcus carry out the experiment described in Exercise 2.3B. They find that more of salt X than salt Y can be dissolved in water at room temperature.

The boys then investigate the solubility of these two salts at different temperatures. The graph shows the results of their investigation.

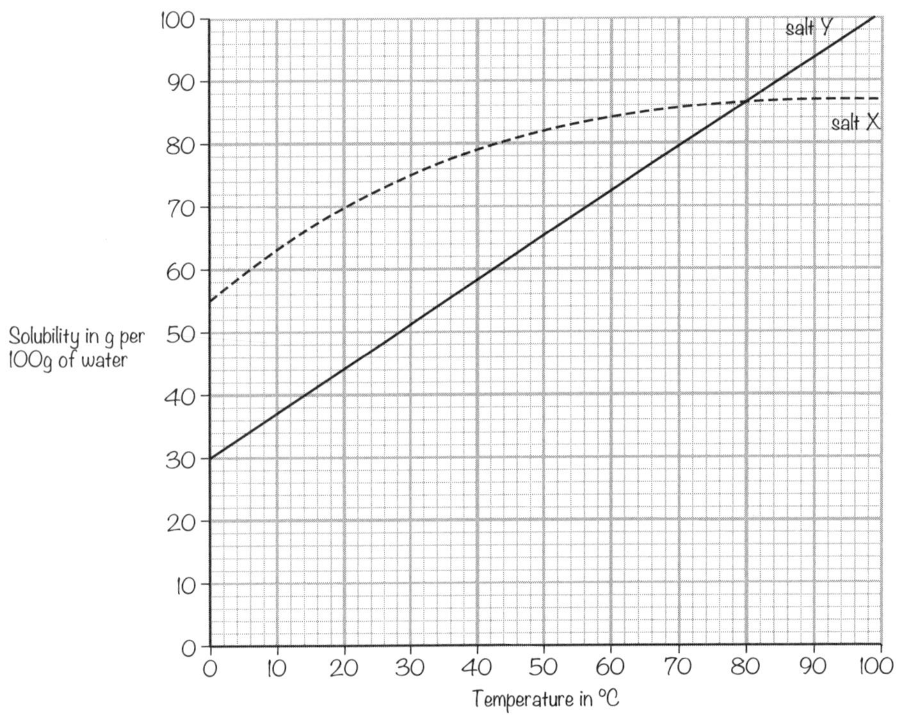

5 At what temperature do the two salts have the same solubility?

....

6 Which salt is less soluble at 50 °C? ....

7 Describe what the graph shows about the solubility of salt X.

....

....

....

8 Describe what the graph shows about the solubility of salt Y.

....

....

....

....

2.4 Paper chromatography

Exercise 2.4A Wordsearch

Focus

This wordsearch contains seven words that are used throughout this unit. Find the words and draw a line around each of them.

M	O	L	E	N	R	O	C	E	L	O	J	F	L
B	S	O	L	U	T	E	T	S	C	G	W	T	X
S	O	L	A	Y	A	L	K	A	S	L	P	I	E
N	L	C	H	R	O	M	A	T	O	G	R	A	M
I	U	T	I	O	N	G	I	U	L	R	K	C	K
E	T	U	D	E	R	M	O	R	P	A	I	M	T
D	I	L	U	T	E	B	R	A	E	P	A	T	E
S	O	L	V	E	N	T	A	T	M	H	S	E	A
U	N	P	R	Y	R	N	X	E	L	F	K	S	K
V	D	E	M	S	A	W	C	D	S	J	A	S	H
D	I	K	D	I	S	S	O	L	V	E	T	M	T
F	L	O	D	B	I	B	C	A	C	L	H	I	X

Exercise 2.4B Paper chromatography

Practice

This exercise will give you practice in interpreting a chromatogram.

A food scientist is testing the food colouring used in drinks sold for children. She has to check that any colouring used does not contain any banned chemical.

She places drops of the drink on chromatography paper. She uses water to allow the colouring to separate.

She also makes another chromatogram of all the permitted chemical colourings. If she finds anything that does not match with these colourings, she will have to carry out further tests.

The diagrams show her two chromatograms.

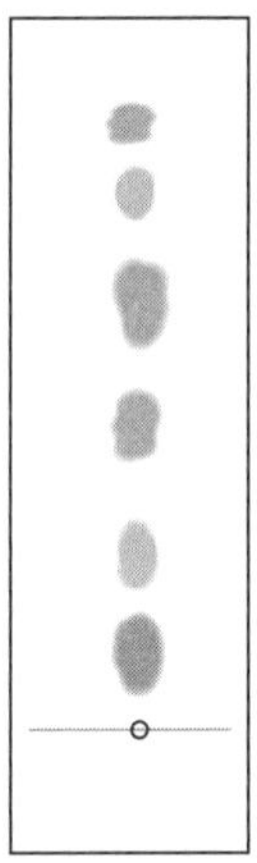

chromatogram from the drink

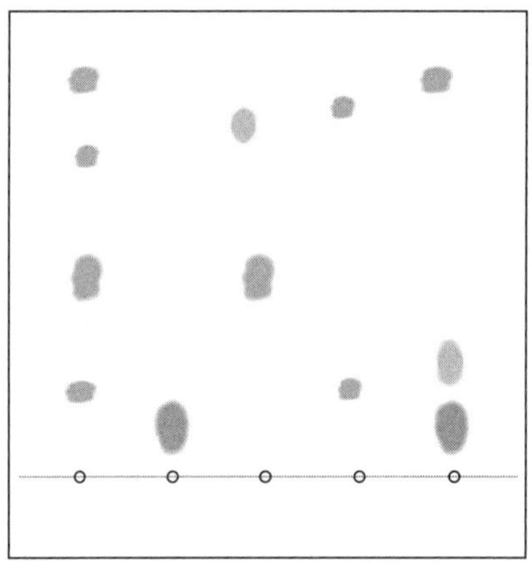

chromatogram of the permitted chemicals

1 Why is the spot of drink placed above the water line at the start of the process?

....

....

2 How many different colourings has the scientist found in the drink?

....

3 Draw a circle around the dye in the drink that is **not** on the permitted list of colourings.

4 Explain why the scientist should carry out further tests on the colouring that you identified in question 3.

....

....

Exercise 2.4C Paper chromatography with plant material

Challenge

This exercise will give you practice in interpreting a chromatogram.

Sofia has been given some liquid that has been extracted from the petals of a flower. She wants to find out if it is a pure substance or if it is a mixture. She places drops of the liquid on a piece of chromatography paper. The diagram shows what she did.

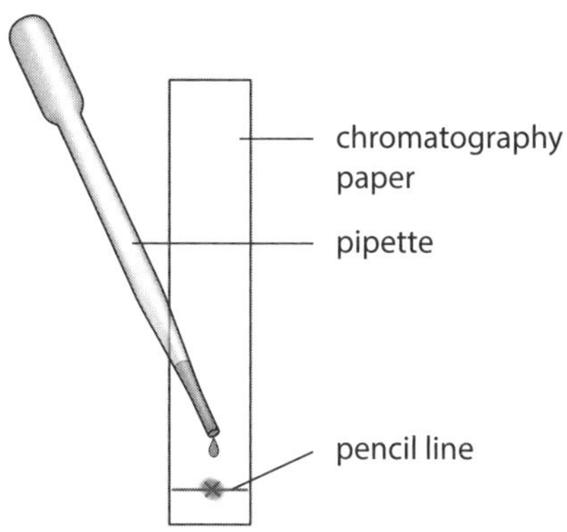

She was careful to allow each drop of liquid to dry before adding another drop. She placed the paper into a beaker containing water and waited to see the result.

After about 15 minutes she saw that the water had moved up the paper but the drop of liquid had not.

1 Explain why this happened.

....

....

2 What should Sofia try now?

....

....

....

....

After Sofia changed her investigation, she produced this chromatogram.

3 Label the chromatogram.

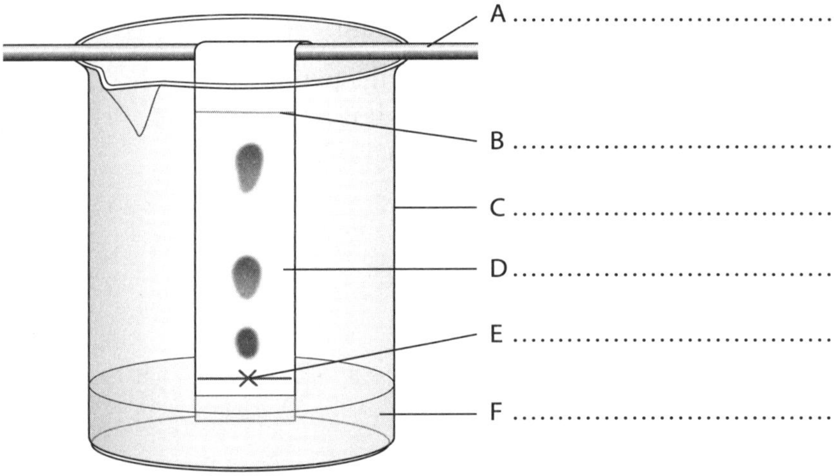

4 Why did Sofia dry the drops of liquid before she added more?

....

....

....

5 Is the liquid extracted from the petals pure or a mixture?
How do you know this?

....

....

....

6 Explain how the liquid was separated.

....

....

....

....

....

....

3 Forces and energy

› 3.1 Forces and motion

Exercise 3.1A Balanced forces

Focus

In this exercise, you will describe balanced forces.

1 What is needed for two forces to be balanced?

Tick (✓) **two** statements in the table.

Statement	Needed for forces to be balanced?
Two forces must be the same size.	
Two forces must be different sizes.	
Two forces must be in the same direction.	
Two forces must be in opposite directions.	

2 A box sits on the ground. The box is **not** moving.

Write 'true' or 'false' after each statement.

a There are no forces acting on the box. ....

b There are balanced forces acting on the box. ....

c There is an unbalanced force acting on the box. ....

3 Sofia is riding her bicycle. The driving force on the bicycle is balanced with the force of friction on the bicycle.

Draw arrows on the diagram to show these forces. Write the names of the forces on the arrows.

Exercise 3.1B Unbalanced forces

Practice skills

In this exercise, you will be thinking about the effects of unbalanced forces.

1 Which of these can happen because of unbalanced forces?

Tick (✓) **all** correct statements.

A car will move at a constant speed. ☐

A boat will slow down. ☐

A football will change direction. ☐

A book will not move on a desk. ☐

2 The diagram shows the forces on a car.

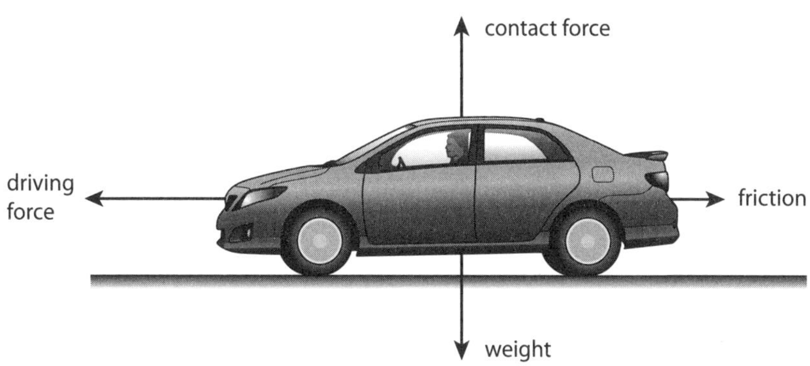

State:

a which forces are balanced

.... and ....

b which forces are unbalanced

.... and ....

c what will happen to the car.

....

Exercise 3.1C Changing direction

Challenge

In this exercise, you will describe how unbalanced forces can cause a change in direction of movement.

1 The diagram shows the forces, A–D, acting on a bird when it is flying.

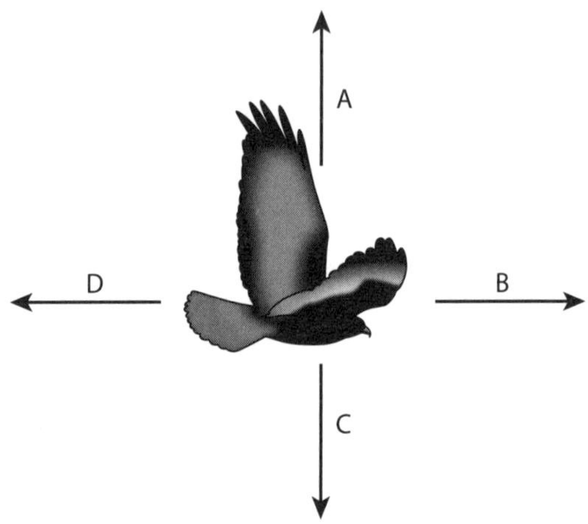

a Describe the effects of these forces on the movement of the bird.

....

....

....

b Describe **one** change needed to the forces for the bird to go higher.

....

c Describe **two** changes to the forces that would make the bird go slower.

1 ....

2 ....

2 An aeroplane is flying north, in a straight line, at a constant speed.

The aeroplane needs to turn towards east.

Draw an arrow on the diagram to show the direction of the unbalanced force needed to make the aeroplane turn east.

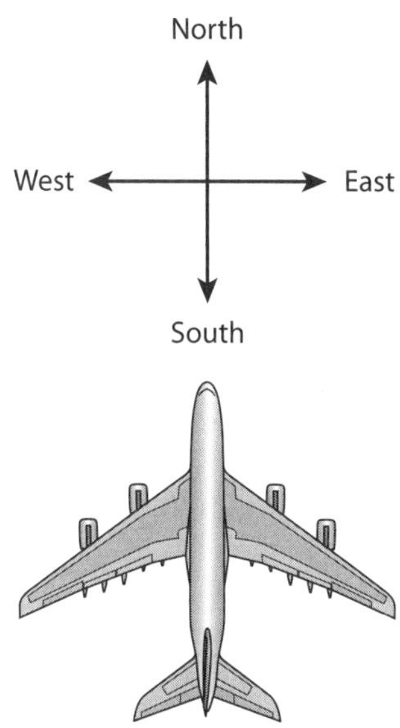

3 Tetherball is a game. A tennis ball is attached to a string. The string can rotate around a vertical pole. The tennis ball moves in a circle around the pole.

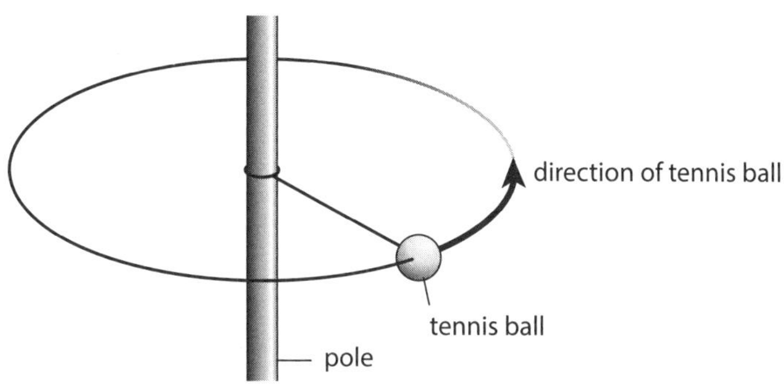

The tennis ball in the diagram is moving in the direction shown.

a Draw an arrow on the diagram to show the direction of the unbalanced force on the tennis ball. Label this arrow F.

b The string breaks when the tennis ball is at the position shown.

Draw another arrow on the diagram to show the direction that the tennis ball will move when the string breaks. Label this arrow D.

3.2 Speed

Exercise 3.2A Units of speed

Focus

In this exercise, you will consider the units of speed.

1 a Which of these is the standard unit of distance in science?

Circle **one** unit.

metre **foot** **mile** **kilometre**

b Which of these is the standard unit of time in science?

Circle **one** unit.

day **hour** **minute** **second**

c Which of these is the standard unit for speed in science?

Circle **one** unit.

m s **m/s** **m/s^2** **m^{2}s**

2 Speed can be measured in kilometres per hour, km/h.

A motorcycle travels at 60 km/h.

What does 60 km/h mean?

Tick (✓) **one** box.

It travels a distance of 60 m every second. ☐

It travels a distance of 60 m every hour. ☐

It travels a distance of 60 km every second. ☐

It travels a distance of 60 km every hour. ☐

3 In the year 2016, a spacecraft reached a speed of 260 000 km/h.

Calculate the distance this spacecraft would travel in 2 hours.

Show your working.

.... km

Exercise 3.2B Calculating speed

Practice

In this exercise, you will calculate the speeds of some objects.

1 a Write the equation that links speed, distance and time.

b Give the unit of speed when distance is in metres and time is in seconds.

....

In each of these calculations, show your working **and** give the unit with your answer.

2 A car travels a distance of 70 m in a time of 2 s.

a Calculate the average speed of the car.

....

The car changes speed to travel a distance of 30 m in a time of 2 s.

b Calculate the new speed of the car.

....

3 Arun walks from home to school. School is a distance of 450 m from Arun's home.

Arun walks this distance in a time of 300 s.

a Calculate Arun's average walking speed.

....

b Explain why your answer to part **a** is an average speed.

....

....

4 An aeroplane travels a distance of 5400 km in a time of 6 hours.

Calculate the average speed of the aeroplane, in km/h.

....

Exercise 3.2C Calculating distance and time

Challenge

In this exercise, you will use speed to calculate either the distance or the time of travel.

1 a Complete the equation for calculating distance from speed and time.

distance = ...

b Complete the equation for calculating time of travel from speed and distance.

time = ...

In each of these calculations, show your working **and** give the unit with your answer.

2 A train travels at a constant speed of 45 m/s.

a Calculate the distance travelled by the train in:

i 30 s

....

ii 2 minutes.

....

3 Zara runs at a constant speed of 4 m/s.

Sofia rides her bicycle at a constant speed of 6 m/s.

a Calculate the time taken for Zara to run a distance of 120 m.

....

b Calculate how much further Sofia travels in one minute than Zara does.

....

4 Marcus's father plans to travel by car. He needs to travel a distance of 50 km in a time of 2 hours.

a Calculate the average speed at which the car must travel.

....

b Explain why the car must go faster than your answer to part **a** for some parts of the journey.

....

....

....

3.3 Describing movement

Exercise 3.3A Distance/time graphs 1

Focus

In this exercise, you will decide what you can work out from a distance/time graph.

1 Which of these can be worked out from a distance/time graph?

Tick (✓) **one** box.

The force on an object. ☐
The speed of an object. ☐
The mass of an object. ☐
The weight of an object. ☐

2 Look at the distance/time graph for a train.

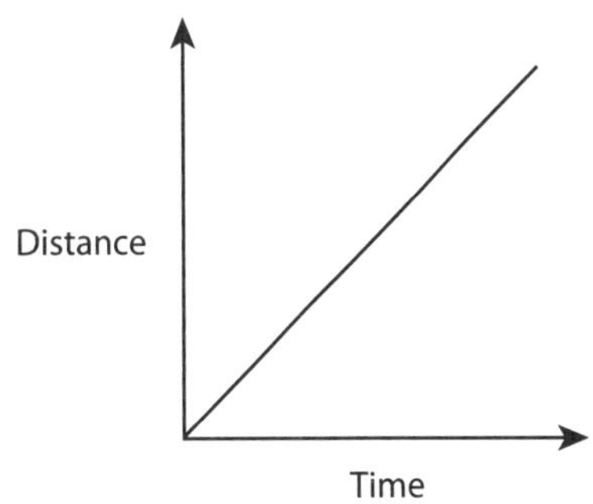

a Which of these distance/time graphs shows the train going faster?

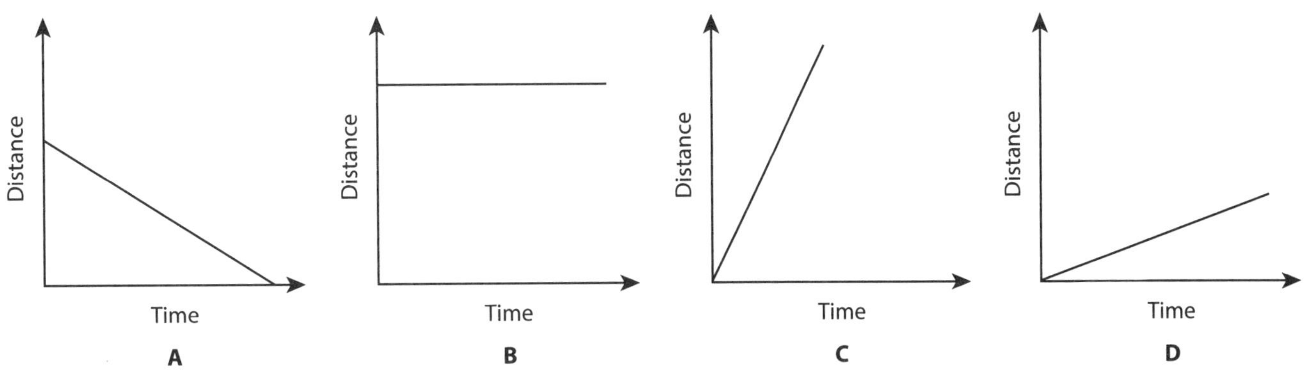

Write the letter. ....

b Which distance/time graph in part **a** shows **no** change in distance with time?

Write the letter. ....

Exercise 3.3B Distance/time graphs 2

Practice

In this exercise, you will sketch some distance/time graphs.

When sketching a graph, you only label the axes with quantities. You do **not** need to scale the axes **or** put numbers on the axes.

1 Sketch a distance/time graph for:

a a stationary object

b an object travelling at a constant speed away from a starting position

c an object travelling at a constant speed back towards its starting position.

2 Sofia walks from home to a shop.

She walks at a constant low speed.

She stops to talk to a friend.

She continues walking to the shop at a higher speed than before.

Sketch a distance/time graph of Sofia's journey from home to the shop.

3 Marcus rides a bicycle at a constant speed from the park to a friend's house.

Marcus stays at his friend's house for a short time.

Marcus rides his bicycle at the same constant speed back again from his friend's house to the park.

Sketch a distance/time graph of Marcus's journey from the park and back to the park. Label the vertical axis 'distance from park'.

Exercise 3.3C Distance/time graphs 3

Challenge

In this exercise, you will draw a distance/time graph and work out values from the graph.

1 An aeroplane departs from airport A at time 0 hours.

The aeroplane takes 4.5 hours to travel to airport B.

Airport B is a distance of 3600 km away from airport A.

The aeroplane spends 1.5 hours at airport B, before departing again for airport A.

The journey back from airport B to airport A takes 4.0 hours.

a Draw a distance/time graph of the journey on the grid below.

Label the vertical axis 'distance from A'.

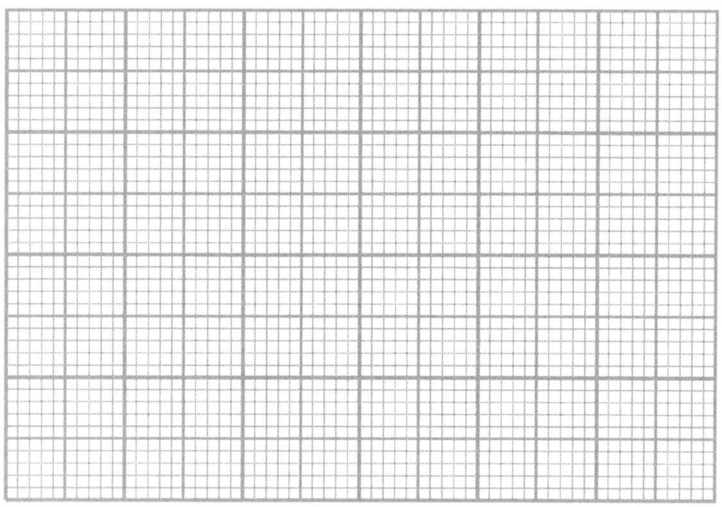

b Use your graph to work out:

i the total time of the journey

....

ii the speed of the aeroplane going from airport A to airport B

....

iii the speed of the aeroplane going from airport B to airport A.

....

3.4 Turning forces

Exercise 3.4A Identifying turning forces

Focus

In this exercise, you will decide where turning forces are used.

1 Which of these actions needs a turning force to happen?

Tick (✓) **all** that apply.

- pushing a door open ☐
- pulling a chair across the floor ☐
- twisting the top off a bottle ☐
- pushing the hands of a clock around ☐
- pushing a trolley up a ramp ☐
- stretching an elastic band ☐

2 Which of these objects needs a turning force to work?

Tick (✓) **all** that apply.

☐

☐

☐

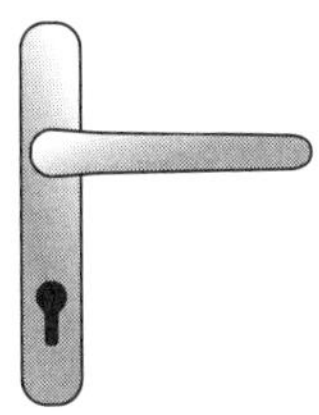
☐

☐

3 What name is given to the turning effect of a force?

Circle **one** word.

minute **moment** **rotate** **revolve**

Exercise 3.4B Calculating moments

Practice

In this exercise, you will calculate moments and make predictions about moments.

1 Write the equation that links moment, force and distance.

....

2 The picture shows a crane supporting a 15 000 N weight.

The weight is supported 5 m from the pivot of the crane.

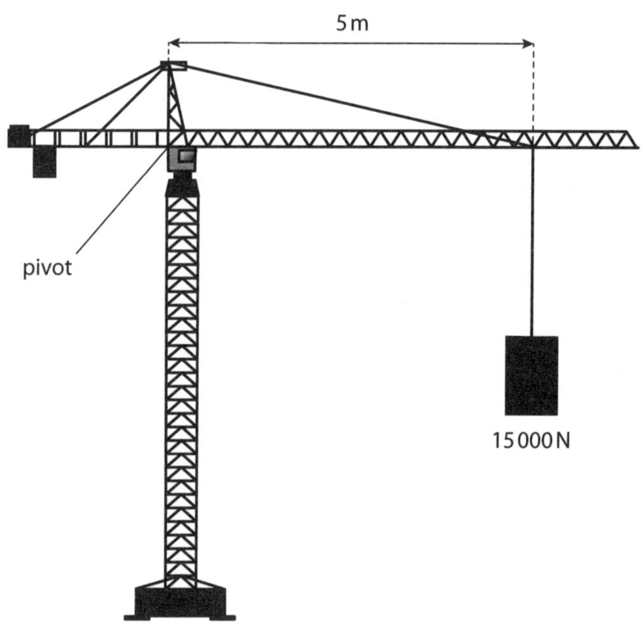

a Calculate the moment caused by the weight on the crane.

Show your working.

.... N m

b Explain the effect on this moment of:

i moving the weight further from the pivot

....

....

ii moving the weight closer to the pivot.

....

....

3 Some people use units that are **not** international standard units.

One of these units of force is pounds.

One of these units of distance is the foot.

Write the unit of moment in these units.

....

Exercise 3.4C Moments, force and distance

Challenge

In this exercise, you will calculate forces and distances for moments.

1 A spanner will turn a nut. The nut needs a moment of 40 N m to turn. The spanner is 0.2 m long.

a Calculate the **minium** force that must be exerted on the spanner.

Show your working and give the unit.

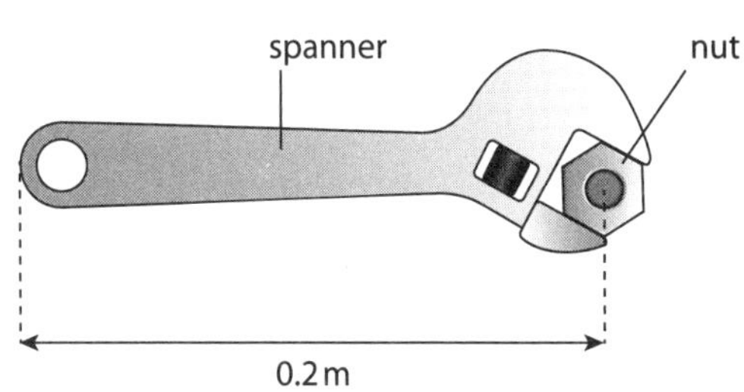

....

b Explain why using a longer spanner will make the nut easier to turn.

....

....

2 An engine exerts a moment of 350 N m when measured at a wheel.

The engine drives a wheel that has a radius of 0.35 m.

The pivot of the wheel is at the centre.

Calculate the force at the outside of the wheel.

Show your working and give the unit.

....

3 Sofia weighs 500 N. She sits on a seesaw at a distance of 2 m from the pivot.

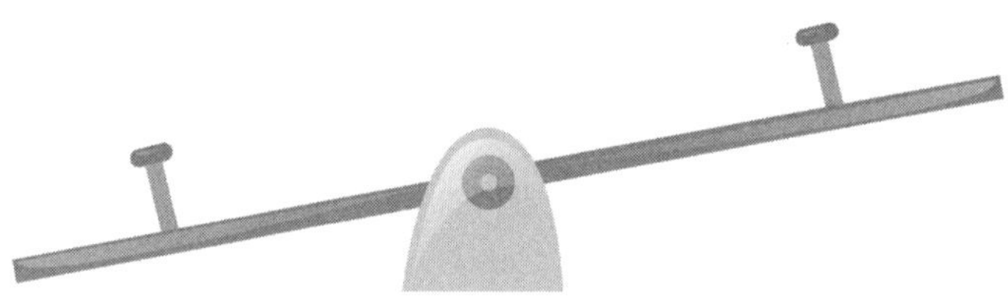

a Calculate the moment that Sofia exerts on the seesaw.

Show your working and give the unit.

....

b The seesaw will balance when the moments on both sides are equal.

Zara weighs 400 N.

Calculate the distance from the pivot to where Zara should sit to balance the seesaw.

Show your working and give the unit.

....

3.5 Pressure between solids

Exercise 3.5A Describing pressure

Focus

In this exercise, you will describe what affects pressure in solids.

1 Which of these is used to work out pressure?

Tick (✓) **one** box.

$\text{pressure} = \frac{\text{force}}{\text{area}}$	☐	$\text{pressure} = \text{mass} \times \text{area}$	☐
$\text{pressure} = \frac{\text{mass}}{\text{area}}$	☐	$\text{pressure} = \text{force} \times \text{area}$	☐

2 Zara has four different styles of shoes.

Which shoes will exert the greatest pressure on the floor when Zara wears them?

Tick (✓) **one** box.

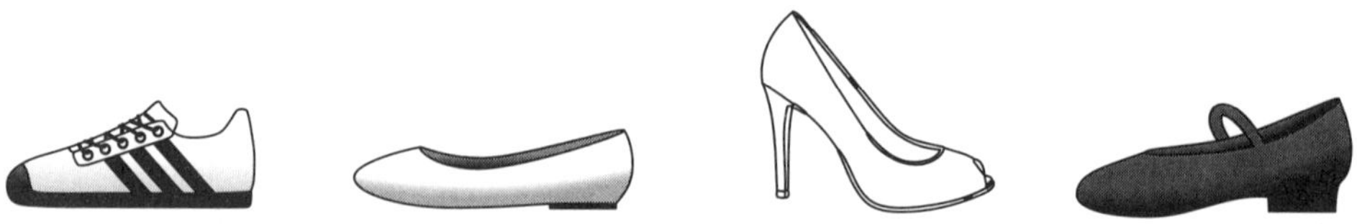

☐ ☐ ☐ ☐

3 The picture shows a box. The areas of three faces of the box, A, B and C, are shown.

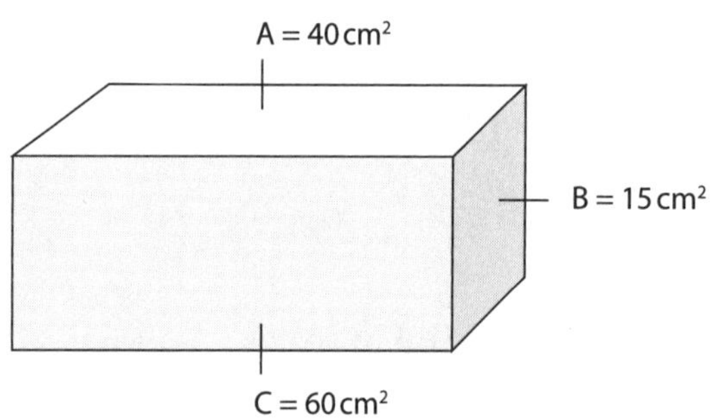

a Which face of the box will exert the **smallest** pressure on the floor?

Write the letter. ....

b Explain your answer to part **a**.

....

....

Exercise 3.5B Calculating pressure

Practice

In this exercise, you will calculate pressure in solids and think about the units of pressure.

1 A rock exerts a pressure of 20 N/cm^2 on the ground.

What does 20 N/cm^2 mean?

Complete the sentence.

A force of .... acts on each .... of area.

2 A large book has a weight of 15 N. The area of one end of the book is 60 cm^2.

Calculate the pressure the book exerts when standing on this end.

Show your working.

.... N/cm^2

3 A nail will go into wood if the pressure on the end of the nail is 60 N/mm^2.

The area of the end of the nail in contact with the wood is 0.5 mm^2.

Calculate the force needed on the nail to make it go into the wood.

Show your working and give the unit with your answer.

....

4 Not all of the units used by people are standard scientific units. Some people use other units.

One of these other units of force is pounds.

One of these other units of area is square inch.

State the unit of pressure in these other units.

....

Exercise 3.5C Variables affecting pressure

Challenge

In this exercise, you will consider the variables that affect pressure in solids.

1 The picture shows part of the stem of a plant called a rose.
The stem has parts called thorns.

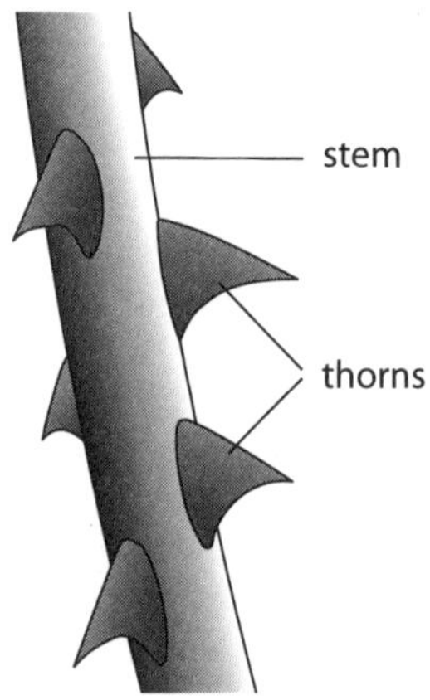

Explain, in terms of pressure, why touching the thorns is more likely to cause injury than touching other parts of the stem.

....

....

....

2 Cars can get stuck in sand when a wheel sinks down into the sand.

Explain why putting a large piece of wood under the wheel can stop the wheel from sinking.

....

....

....

3 Arun is cutting bread.

Explain why a sharp knife is better for cutting bread than a knife that is **not** sharp.

....

....

....

4 The picture shows a drawing pin. The two ends of the drawing pin are labelled A and B.

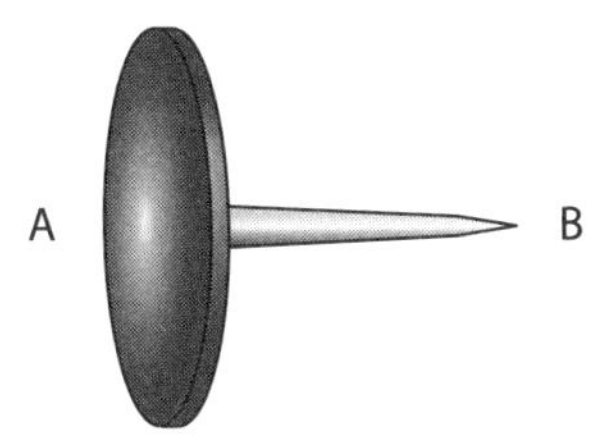

Part A is pushed by your thumb.

Part B goes into a wall or drawing board.

Explain the shape of each end of the drawing pin.

....

....

....

....

› 3.6 Pressure in liquids and gases

Exercise 3.6A Trends in pressure 1

Focus

In this exercise, you will describe what affects pressure in liquids and gases.

1 **Extension material:** State what happens to the pressure in a liquid as depth increases.

....

2 **Extension material:** Where is pressure in the air largest?

Tick (✓) **one** box.

at sea level ☐

at the top of a mountain ☐

at the top of clouds ☐

at the top of the atmosphere ☐

3 A car tyre is filled with air.

When the car is moving, the temperature of the tyre increases.

State what happens to the pressure of the air in the tyre when temperature increases.

....

4 A plastic bottle is filled with air. The top is on the bottle so the air **cannot** escape.

The bottle is squeezed so the volume decreases.

State what happens to the pressure of the air in the bottle when the volume decreases.

....

Exercise 3.6B Trends in pressure 2

Practice

In this exercise, you will think in more detail about what affects pressure in liquids and gases.

1 The picture shows a small fish in deep water. The fish is **not** moving. The water is **not** moving.

The arrows A, B and C show three directions from which pressure from the water acts on the fish.

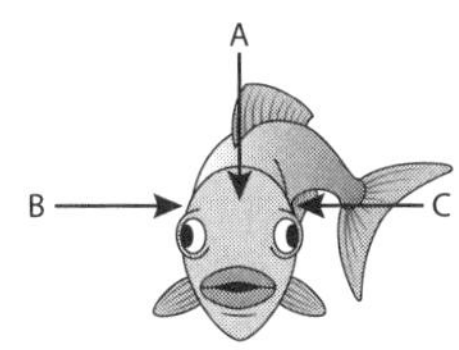

Which statement is correct?

Tick (✓) **one** box.

The pressure in direction A is the largest. ☐

The pressure in direction B is the largest. ☐

The pressure in direction C is the largest. ☐

The pressure is equal in all directions. ☐

2 The picture shows water coming out of three holes in a bottle.

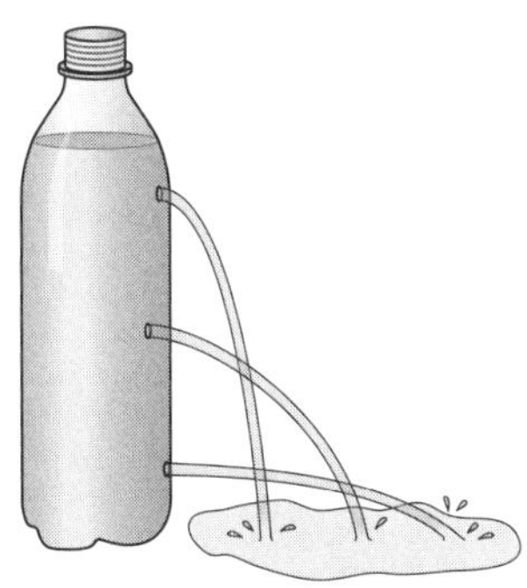

Describe the conclusion that can be made from this observation.

....

....

3 A balloon is filled with air. The balloon is then sealed so that air **cannot** escape.

a State what will happen to the pressure inside the balloon if the temperature decreases.

....

b Explain your answer to part **a**.

....

....

....

Exercise 3.6C Trends in pressure 3 (extension material)

Challenge

In this exercise, you will demonstrate understanding of changes in pressure in gases.

1 A balloon is filled with air. The balloon is then sealed so that air **cannot** escape.

The diameter of the balloon is 20 cm.

Very cold liquid is poured over the balloon.

The balloon becomes smaller until its diameter is 5 cm.

Explain this observation.

....

....

....

....

....

2 The tyres on an aeroplane are filled with nitrogen gas.

The aeroplane is at an altitude of 11 000 m. The temperature of the tyres is −50°C.

The aeroplane lands on the ground 30 minutes later.
The temperature of the tyres is now 25°C.

a Sketch a graph to show the change in atmospheric pressure outside the aeroplane during this 30 minute period.

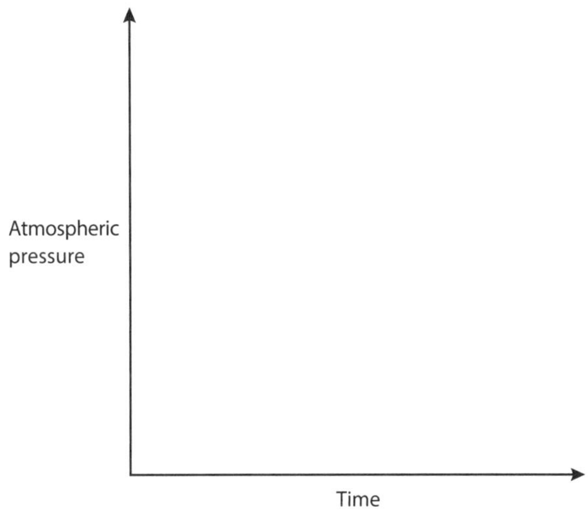

b Sketch a graph to show the change in gas pressure inside the tyres during this 30-minute period.

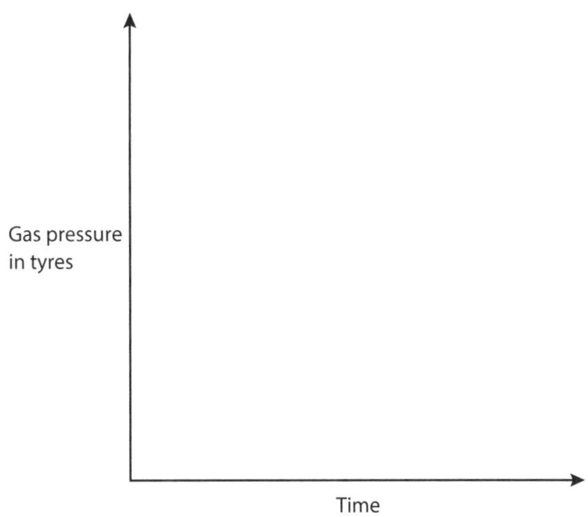

3.7 Particles on the move

Exercise 3.7A Diffusion in gases and liquids

Focus

In this exercise, you will describe what happens when gases mix and when liquids mix.

1 Two glass jars are kept apart with a seal.

One jar contains a coloured gas.

The other jar contains a colourless gas.

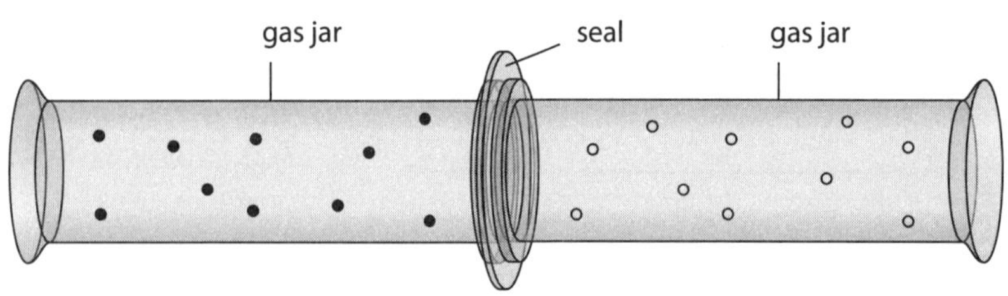

The seal is removed.

Draw the arrangement of particles in the jars some time after the seal was removed.

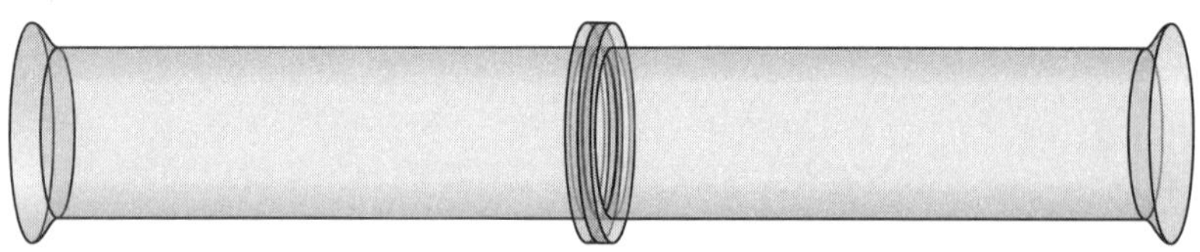

2 A small volume of coloured ink is placed into a beaker of water.

The diagram shows the particles in the ink just after adding to the water. The ink dissolves in the water.

Draw the arrangement of ink particles in the water a long time after the ink was added.

Exercise 3.7B Diffusion

Practice

In this exercise, you will describe diffusion in terms of particle movement in gases and liquids.

1 Describe what is meant by diffusion.

....

....

....

2 A small volume of blue ink is added to a beaker of water.

There is blue colour only at the bottom of the beaker.

a Explain why the water eventually all turns blue.

....

....

....

b Explain why the water turns blue faster when the temperature of the water is higher.

....

....

3 Bromine is a brown liquid that evaporates easily at room temperature.

When a container of bromine is opened, brown gas comes out of the container.

Explain why the colour of the brown gas becomes less intense as it gets further away from the container.

....

....

....

4 A green gas is added to a bottle that contains air.

A short time later, the green colour has spread to fill the bottle.

Write **true** or **false** next to each statement.

When the green colour fills the bottle, the movement of particles has stopped. ....

When the green colour fills the bottle, diffusion has stopped.

....

Exercise 3.7C Variables affecting diffusion

Challenge

In this exercise, you will think of variables that affect the speed of diffusion.

1 A purple crystal is added into the bottom of a large beaker of water.

When the crystal dissolves, the liquid turns purple.

Eventually, all the liquid is purple.

a Explain why the purple colour is more intense when the crystal first dissolves and less intense when it has spread through all the liquid.

....

....

....

Stirring speeds up the spreading of the purple colour.

b List **two other** changes that would speed up the spreading of the purple colour.

1 ....

2 ....

2 Sofia makes two cups of coffee. One is cold and the other is hot.

The cups and the coffee are the same in all other ways.

Zara says that the hot coffee has a stronger smell than the cold coffee.

Explain why this is the case.

....

....

....

3 Many animals use smell to find food.

Explain how these animals know what direction to move to get to the food.

....

....

....

4 Ecosystems

› 4.1 The Sonoran Desert

Exercise 4.1 The Sonoran Desert ecosystem

In this exercise, you will practise finding and using information in a written passage. You will think about different habitats in an ecosystem. You will also consider how different species interact with each other in an ecosystem, and how the loss of one species could affect others.

Focus

Saguaro cacti are found only in the Sonoran Desert in Arizona, USA. They can live to be 200 years old.

Saguaro cacti grow in dry places, where it rains only occasionally. Their roots spread out widely, just below the soil surface. This means that they can capture a lot of water when it rains.

They do not have leaves, because water would evaporate from them. The plant would dry out. Instead, the cactus uses its green stems to make food by photosynthesis.

Saguaro cacti cannot grow in places where the temperature falls below 0°C. Their cells are killed if they freeze.

There are sharp spines on the cactus stems, which protect them from being eaten by animals.

1 Describe the habitat of the saguaro cactus.

....

....

2 Describe **two** ways in which the saguaro cactus is adapted to live in this habitat.

....

....

....

....

3 It is much colder on the mountains than in the desert. Explain why saguaro cacti cannot grow on the high mountains.

....

....

Practice

Saguaro cacti provide habitats and food for other species in the desert. Some species of birds, including Gila woodpeckers and gilded flickers, use their beaks to make nest holes in the cactus's stems. After these birds have left the nest, other birds such as elf owls use the holes. Harris hawks make their nests of sticks where the arms of the cactus branch from the main stem.

The cactus flowers produce pollen and nectar. These are eaten by bats, which pollinate the flowers. The flowers produce fruits after they have been pollinated. The fruits are eaten by birds, mammals and reptiles such as desert tortoises.

4 Use this information to suggest how the Sonoran Desert ecosystem would be affected if:

- all the Gila woodpeckers and gilded flickers died out

....

....

....

....

- all the saguaro cacti died out.

....

....

....

....

Challenge

Many parts of Arizona have plenty of rainfall. They provide habitats for many different species of plant.

5 Suggest why saguaro cacti do not grow in these wetter areas.

....

....

....

....

4.2 Different ecosystems

Exercise 4.2A A tropical rainforest ecosystem

Focus

This exercise gives you practice in using the correct words when you are writing about ecosystems and habitats.

Complete the sentences. Use each of these words once only.

decomposers ecosystem environment habitats nutrients

Tropical rainforests grow where the temperature is always high and there is plenty of rainfall. Many different species of plant grow in the rainforest.

The rainforest provides .... and food for many different species of animal.

On the forest floor, fungi break down dead leaves and waste from the animals. These fungi are ....

The fungi release .... from the dead leaves and waste, which help the plants to grow.

All of the plants, animals and fungi interact with one another. They also interact with the non-living parts of their ....

This network of interactions makes up the tropical rainforest

....

Exercise 4.2B Hydrothermal vents

Practice

In this exercise, you will think about a very unusual ecosystem. You will use information to construct a food chain, and think about the different habitats in the ecosystem.

In 1977, a completely new ecosystem was discovered. In the deep ocean, below the surface, scientists found places where hot water rushes out from the sea bed into the water.

These places are called hydrothermal vents. 'Hydro' means water, 'thermal' means heat, and a vent is an opening that things can pass through.

No one expected to find any life at a hydrothermal vent. It is completely dark. The water temperature can be as high as 400 °C where it pours out, although it cools as it mixes with the sea water.

But the scientists found many living organisms in this strange ecosystem. Instead of plants, tiny bacteria are the producers in the food chain. Instead of using energy from light to make food, they use energy in the chemicals dissolved in the hot water. The bacteria are able to survive in much higher temperatures than most living things.

Giant tube worms also live at hydrothermal vents. Some of the bacteria live inside the tube worms. The worms provide a habitat for the bacteria, and use some of the food that the bacteria make.

Other bacteria live in the hot water around the vent. They form thick mats on the sea floor. The bacteria are eaten by shrimps and tiny floating animals called zooplankton. The zooplankton are eaten by sea anemones. Crabs and octopuses eat sea anemones and tube worms.

1 Explain why plants cannot live at a hydrothermal vent.

....

....

....

....

2 Construct a food chain, containing four types of organism, that occurs at a hydrothermal vent.

3 Name the producer in your food chain.

....

4 Where does this producer obtain its energy from?

....

5 Describe **two** different habitats in the hydrothermal vent ecosystem.

....

....

Exercise 4.2C Mangroves and fish

Challenge

In this exercise, you will read about an experiment to find out how one ecosystem can affect another. The first ecosystem is a mangrove forest, and the second is a coral reef. You will also practise using data to draw conclusions.

Mangroves are trees that grow on muddy seashores in tropical regions. Their roots are covered by sea water when the tide is high. Mangroves have unusual root systems that help to support them in the mud.

The mangrove ecosystem provides habitats for many different animals. Baby fish often spend their early lives amongst the mangrove roots, safe from predators such as larger fish.

Ecologists wanted to find out whether the presence of mangroves affected the numbers of fish in nearby coral reef ecosystems. They collected samples of four species of fish on several coral reefs where there were mangroves on the shore, and on several coral reefs where there were no mangroves. They measured the mass of each fish.

The table shows their results. The mass is given in kg/km^2. This means the number of kilograms of that kind of fish in an area of one kilometre squared of coral reef.

Species of fish	Mass of fish on coral reef in kg/km^2	
	Mangroves on the shore	No mangroves on the shore
striped parrotfish	2170	1530
blue-striped grunt	447	288
yellowtail	6715	3098
schoolmaster	1898	1767

1 Explain the meaning of each of these words.

habitat

....

ecosystem

....

predator

....

2 Which species of fish has the largest mass on coral reefs where there are mangroves on the shore?

....

3 Describe how the masses of fish on coral reefs where there are no mangroves on the shore differ from coral reefs where there are mangroves on the shore.

....

....

....

4 Suggest reasons for the difference that you have described in your answer to question 3.

....

....

....

....

4.3 Intruders in an ecosystem

Exercise 4.3A Beavers in South America

Focus

This exercise is about an invasive species in South America. You need to read the information carefully, then write answers in your own words.

Beavers are mammals that live in streams and rivers in North America. They have thick, soft, waterproof fur.

Beavers make dams in rivers. The dams slow down the river water and form deep, wide pools. Beavers use their sharp teeth to cut down trees to build their dams.

1 What is the habitat of beavers?

....

2 Describe how beavers change the habitat that they live in.

....

....

....

In 1946, some beavers were taken to Tierra del Fuego in South America, to breed for their fur.

Today, no beavers are used for fur. But the beavers still live in Tierra del Fuego. The numbers of beavers have increased. Their dams have caused a lot of damage to local ecosystems.

3 In North America, beavers are killed and eaten by brown bears. Some people have suggested introducing brown bears to Tierra del Fuego, to control the beavers.

Suggest why this might not be a good idea.

....

....

....

....

Exercise 4.3B Water hyacinth

Practice

This exercise is about a plant that has become an invasive species in many different countries. You will practise finding information in a passage. You will combine this information with your own knowledge to answer questions.

Water hyacinths are South American plants that live in fresh water. They have tough, green leaves that float on the water surface. They also have beautiful blue flowers.

In South America, several herbivores feed on water hyacinth. The herbivores help to stop the number of water hyacinth plants increasing too much.

Water hyacinths have been introduced to many countries outside South America. They are an invasive species in many aquatic ecosystems. They have multiplied rapidly, covering vast areas of rivers and lakes. They make such a thick covering that light and oxygen cannot reach the water below. This kills native plants and fish.

On Lake Victoria, in Tanzania and Uganda, there is so much water hyacinth that the fishing boats cannot move through it. The fishing nets catch water hyacinth, not fish.

1 Explain the meaning of each of these words.

herbivore

....

....

invasive species

....

....

aquatic

....

....

2 Explain why water hyacinths are **not** an invasive species in South America.

....

....

....

....

3 Explain **two** ways in which water hyacinth is causing problems in Lake Victoria. Use your own words.

First way

....

....

....

Second way

....

....

....

Exercise 4.3C Cane toads in Australia

Challenge

This exercise is about a new, invasive species in Australia, and the effects that it has had on other organisms in the local ecosystems. You will plan an experiment to find out if a strategy that is trying to save a native predator is working.

Cane toads are huge toads that live naturally in South America.

In 1935, 101 cane toads were brought to northern Australia. This was done because the toads eat beetles that were destroying sugar cane.

The toads bred rapidly. They have now spread to most parts of northern Australia.

Cane toads are poisonous. In South America, they have many predators. These help to keep the numbers of cane toads under control. However, in Australia, predators that eat cane toads often die. This has reduced the numbers of many rare Australian animals, such as the northern quoll.

Scientists in Australia are trying to teach wild northern quolls not to eat cane toads. They are making little sausages of cane toad meat and feeding them to the quolls. This makes the quolls vomit, but does not kill them. The scientists hope that the quolls will learn to avoid cane toads.

1 Suggest why the numbers of cane toads have increased rapidly in Australia, whereas in their native South America the numbers stay fairly constant.

....

....

....

....

....

2 Suggest an experiment that the scientists could do to test this hypothesis:

> Feeding cane toad sausages to northern quolls helps to stop them eating cane toads.

Remember to think about variables that the scientists should change, measure or keep the same.

Predict the results that you would expect if the hypothesis is supported.

....

....

....

....

....

....

....

....

....

....

4.4 Bioaccumulation

Exercise 4.4A Microplastics

In this exercise, you will learn about microplastics. You can try finding information in a bar chart. You will also think about bioaccumulation.

Focus

Microplastics are tiny pieces of plastic less than 5 mm long.

Some microplastics come from big pieces of plastic that people have thrown away, and that slowly break apart. Some microplastics come from healthcare and beauty products such as toothpastes and face creams.

In the sea, microplastics can float in the water. They are accidentally taken into the bodies of living organisms when they feed. Some of the denser microplastics slowly fall to the sea bed.

1 What are microplastics?

....

....

2 Explain where microplastics come from.

....

....

....

3 Explain why some microplastics are found in the mud at the bottom of the sea.

....

....

....

Practice

The graph shows the quantities of microplastics found in the mud at the bottom of the sea in four years between 1996 and 2008.

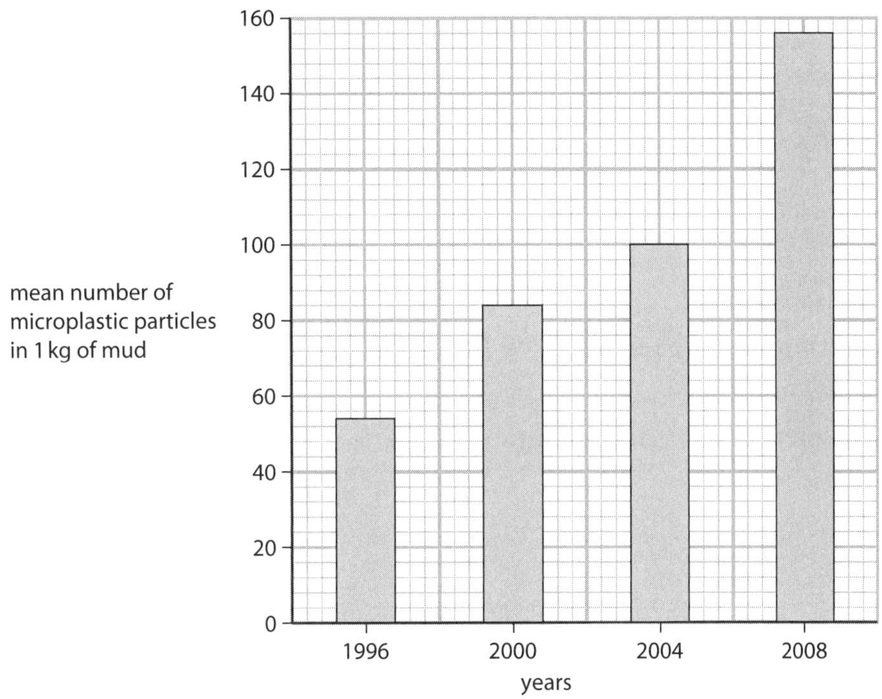

4 Look at the graph.

a State the mean number of microplastic particles found in 1 kg of mud in 1996.

....

b Calculate the increase in the number of microplastic particles in 1 kg of mud between 1996 and 2008.

Show your working.

....

5 Zooplankton are tiny floating organisms that live in the sea. Some fish feed by sucking in sea water and filtering out the zooplankton.

Explain why these fish may end up with microplastics in their bodies.

....

....

....

Challenge

6 Microplastics cannot be broken down by living things. They show bioaccumulation.

Explain what is meant by bioaccumulation.

....

....

....

....

7 Seals eat fish. Explain why the concentration of microplastics in a seal's body may be greater than the concentration in a fish's body.

....

....

....

....

....

Exercise 4.4B Bias

In this exercise you will look at some information and decide if it could be biased.

Focus

Some farmers have noticed that their maize crops are being badly damaged by insect pests that are new to the area. Maize is a very important crop for these farmers as they make most of their money from it.

An agricultural chemical company is advertising a spray that will kill these insects. The chemical company says that the success rate of killing the insects is 90% and that there is only a very slight risk to animals or humans that eat the maize. The farmers do not want to use anything that could be harmful to any animal or person who eats the maize.

The farmers are concerned that the information from the chemical company may be biased.

1 Why do they think the information may be biased?

....

....

Practice

There is another company that breeds and sells predators of these insect pests and they say there is a 100% success rate and that this method of pest control is "environmentally friendly". The company states that these predators are not harmful to other insects and they only feed on this particular species. These predators are not local to the area.

The farmers think this sounds a much better idea.

2 Could this also be biased information? Explain your answer.

....

....

3 What do you think the company means by the term "environmentally friendly"?

....

....

....

4 If the predators of these insect pests do eat other insects, what problems could this cause?

....

....

....

....

Challenge

The farmers contact the government agriculture department, who give the farmers more advice. They explain that the chemical spray is being investigated as it has been linked to deaths of animals that are higher up the food chain. The spray has also been linked to some illness in children who eat crops treated in this way. The advisors also say that the predator option is not fully tested and that there is some evidence that the predator insects do eat other insects, some of which are essential for the ecosystem.

The agriculture department suggest that if the farmers stop growing maize and increase the other crops that they grow, which the insect pests will not eat, then these pests will move away from the area or die as they have no food.

They also tell the farmers that the university is developing a new strain of maize that is resistant to these insect pests. This should be ready for testing for the next planting season.

5 Suggest why the animals higher up the food chain are at more risk of being affected by this chemical spray.

....

....

....

6 Can the farmers be sure that the advice is unbiased?

....

....

....

7 How could they check for bias?

....

....

....

5 Materials and cycles on Earth

> 5.1 The structure of the atom

Exercise 5.1A Labelling the structure of the atom

Focus

In this exercise, you will label a diagram of the structure of an atom and identify facts about the particles in an atom.

1 Label the diagram showing the structure of the atom.
Use the labels given here.

proton **neutron** **electron** **nucleus of the atom**

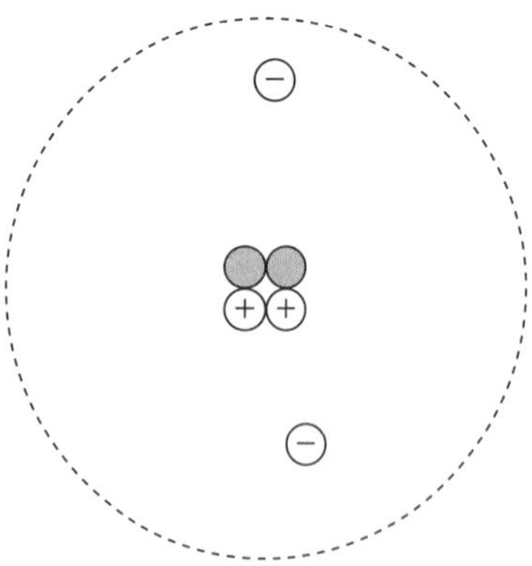

2 What is the white area inside the circle in the diagram?
Label it.

3 Tick (✓) the statements that are correct.

- Electrons have less mass than protons. ☐
- Protons have a negative electrical charge. ☐
- Electrons have a negative electrical charge. ☐
- Neutrons have an electrical charge. ☐
- Neutrons have more mass than electrons. ☐
- Electrons are found in the nucleus of the atom. ☐

Exercise 5.1B Models of the structure of the atom

Practice

In this exercise, you will compare models of the structure of the atom.

1 Draw and label **two** diagrams: one to show J. J. Thompson's model and one to show Rutherford's model of the structure of the atom.

2 Give a difference between J. J. Thompson's model and Rutherford's model of the structure of the atom.

....

....

3 Name another scientist whose work contributed to the model of the atom that is used today.

....

Exercise 5.1C Rutherford's gold foil experiment

Challenge

In this exercise, you will explain what happened in Rutherford's gold foil experiment and what he proved.

1 Complete the diagram to show what happened to the particles when they hit the gold foil.

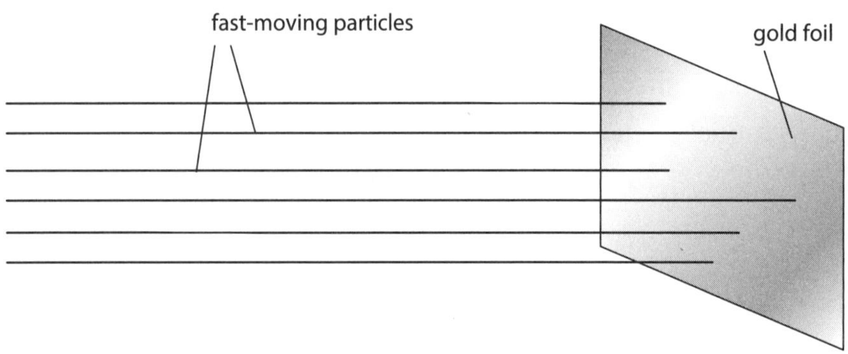

2 What did the results of Rutherford's experiment tell him about the structure of the atom?

....

....

....

....

5.2 Purity

Exercise 5.2 Purity

Focus

In this exercise, you will explain what is meant by 'purity' and calculate the purity of silver.

1 What does a scientist mean by a 'pure element'?

....

....

2 Choose words from the list to complete the paragraph. Each word may be used once, more than once or not at all.

diamonds carbon atoms blue yellow
green nickel hydrogen boron elements
nitrogen compounds most common rarest
coloured colourless

Diamonds are made of .... atoms.

When diamonds are coloured they have .... of different .... mixed in with the carbon atoms.

When they have .... atoms the diamonds will be a blue colour.

If diamonds have nitrogen atoms mixed with the carbon atoms, the diamond will be a .... colour.

The .... colour of diamond is green. Green diamonds have nitrogen, ... or hydrogen mixed in with the carbon atoms.

3 A piece of silver marked 900 tells you that 900 parts out of 1000 of the piece are silver and the rest is made up of other elements. The percentage of silver is calculated as:

$$\frac{900}{1000} \times 100 = 90\%$$

Calculate the percentage of silver in a bracelet marked 925.

......................................%

Practice

In this exercise, you will calculate the purity of gold.

Gold objects are usually marked in carats, to tell you how much gold they contain. A carat stands for one twenty-fourth. So you can work out exactly what percentage of the object is pure gold.

24 carat gold is $24 \times \frac{1}{24} = \frac{24}{24}$

It is twenty-four twenty-fourths gold, so it is pure gold.

To work out the percentage of gold in 24 carat gold:

$$\frac{24}{24} \times 100 = 100\% \text{ gold}$$

18 carat gold is $18 \times \frac{1}{24} = \frac{18}{24}$

It is $\frac{18}{24}$ gold. The remaining six parts are other metals; these are usually copper or silver.

To work out the percentage of gold in 18 carat gold:

$$\frac{18}{24} \times 100 = 75\% \text{ gold}$$

4 **a** Calculate the percentage of gold in 9 carat gold.
Give your answer correct to one decimal place.

.... %

b Calculate the percentage of gold in 22 carat gold.
Give your answer correct to one decimal place.

.... %

c Calculate the percentage of gold in 14 carat gold.
Give your answer correct to one decimal place.

.... %

Challenge

In this exercise, you will practise handling, displaying and interpreting data.

The purity of gold has an effect on how much it costs and also on how hard it is. In Stage 7, you learnt about how alloys are harder than the pure metals.

In a jewellery store, an assistant advises a customer to buy a gold ring that is less than 24 carat. He tells the customer that a ring with a lower proportion of gold looks almost the same as pure gold, but is harder.

Is this true? The table shows some data on the hardness of 'gold'.

Purity of gold alloy in carats	Purity of gold alloy as a percentage	Hardness in arbitrary units
9		80
14		90
18	75	120
22		40
24	100	30

5 Complete the table. The percentages should be correct to one decimal place.

6 Use the information from the table to plot a graph.
Plot the percentage of gold against its hardness.

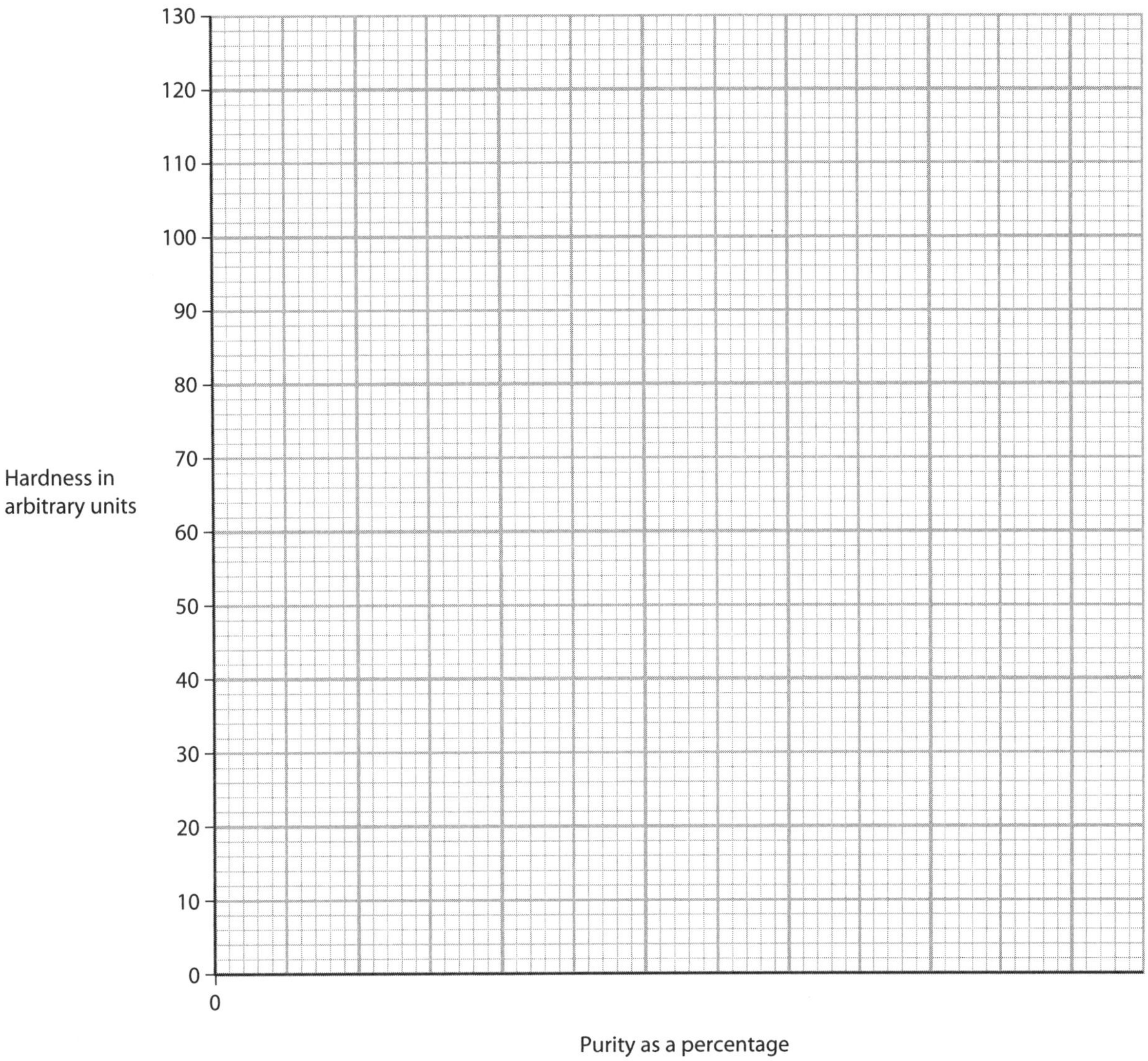

7 Is the advice the assistant gave the customer based on science or opinion? Explain your answer.

....

....

8 Describe the pattern shown by the graph.

....

....

....

9 You may have expected that the 9 carat gold would be harder than the 14 or 18 carat gold. The data show that it is not. Can you suggest why this is so? (Is there another variable, other than the percentage of gold in the alloy, that could be affecting the hardness?)

....

....

....

....

5.3 Weather and climate

Exercise 5.3A Words and meanings

Focus

In this exercise, you will match words with their meanings.

Use a ruler to draw lines to match the words about weather with their meanings.

temperature	rain, hail or snow which falls from clouds
humidity	the layer of gas around the Earth
precipitation	the study of weather
visibility	how hot it is
atmosphere	how far you can see; it depends on the atmospheric conditions or darkness
meteorology	how much water vapour there is in the atmosphere

Exercise 5.3B Weather or climate?

Practice

In this exercise, you will explain the difference between weather and climate and look at different climate zones.

1 Explain the difference between weather and climate.

....

....

....

2 On this map, mark and label the polar zone.

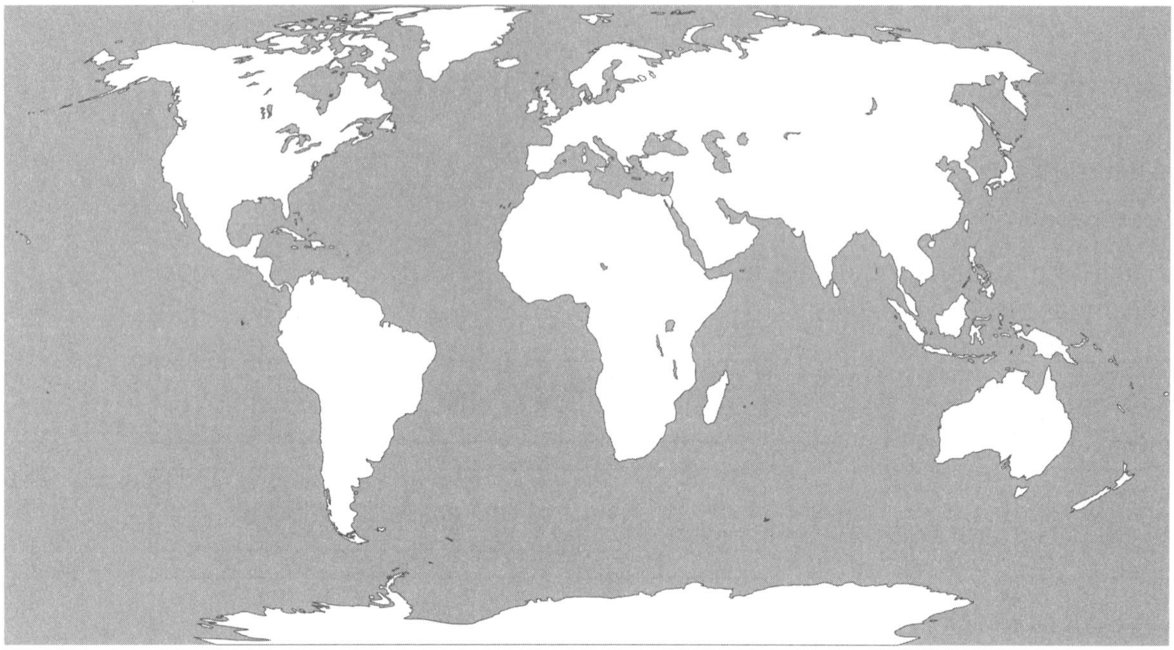

3 Describe the climate in the polar zone.

....

....

4 On the map in question 2, mark and label the tropical zone.

5 Describe the climate in the tropical zone.

....

....

6 Why do meteorologists record the weather in so much detail?

....

....

....

Exercise 5.3C Weather data

Challenge

In this exercise, you will plot and analyse some weather data.

Reykjavik is the capital of Iceland, an island in the North Atlantic Ocean. Iceland is so far north that in the middle of the year, the Sun only sets for a very short time. The table on the following page shows some temperature data taken over one week at the end of July in Reykjavik. The temperature was taken in the same place every six hours.

Date	Time	Temperature in °C
26 July	00:00	13
	06:00	16
	12:00	18
	18:00	19
27 July	00:00	14
	06:00	16
	12:00	18
	18:00	16
28 July	00:00	14
	06:00	16
	12:00	16
	18:00	16
29 July	00:00	14
	06:00	16
	12:00	18
	18:00	17
30 July	00:00	15
	06:00	14
	12:00	18
	18:00	20
31 July	00:00	19
	06:00	19
	12:00	19
	18:00	16
1 August	00:00	14
	06:00	15
	12:00	15
	18:00	14

1 Plot the data onto a graph with the date and times of the four readings for each day along the horizontal axis and the temperatures up the vertical axis. Join the points appropriately.

2 Is there a pattern to each day's temperatures? If so, describe it.

....

....

3 Is there a pattern to the temperature over the whole week? If so, describe it.

....

....

4 It rained heavily on 28 July from 09.00 until 21.00. Do you think this had any effect on the temperature? Explain your answer.

....

....

5 Which climate zone is Iceland in?

....

6 Does the weather this week reflect Iceland's climate zone?

....

....

7 The weather in Iceland usually is very changeable. Can you suggest why this is?

....

....

....

....

....

....

› 5.4 Climate and ice ages

Exercise 5.4A Wordsearch

Focus

This wordsearch contains seven words used throughout this unit. Find the words and draw a line around each of them.

B	O	I	C	V	W	A	H	O	R	D	E	S	D
K	I	C	Y	G	A	B	O	U	L	D	E	R	V
M	L	E	X	B	S	L	S	E	A	G	A	I	C
G	L	A	C	I	E	R	K	I	F	H	O	C	P
N	H	G	L	A	C	I	A	L	M	A	D	E	O
O	U	E	S	Q	G	R	U	H	Y	G	O	S	P
S	D	U	F	B	L	O	P	G	U	E	S	H	E
I	N	T	E	R	G	L	A	C	I	A	L	E	A
P	R	O	D	F	W	O	R	S	H	C	Y	E	T
L	I	E	X	V	U	R	P	N	M	E	Z	T	B
A	M	A	Y	G	O	H	P	D	Y	E	A	O	O
M	A	L	O	C	M	L	A	H	A	B	Z	E	G

Exercise 5.4B Soil cores

Practice

This exercise will give you practice in explaining the use of soil cores.

1 The core of peat has been removed from a bog. Scientists will study the pollen found in the core.

The end nearer to the left of the picture is from the top of the bog.

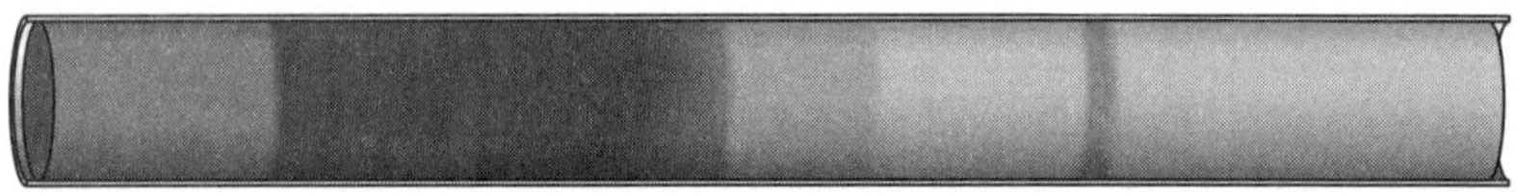

a Is the oldest peat from the top or the bottom of the bog?

....

b Why has the plant material, including pollen, not rotted in the peat bog?

....

....

c What are the scientists hoping to find out by studying the pollen found in the core?

....

....

....

2 a A scientist studies a core that is 956 cm deep. Between 956 cm and 804 cm and between 490 cm and 250 cm she finds pollen from plants that live in cold regions. What are these cold time periods on Earth known as?

....

b In the rest of the core she finds pollen from plants that only live in warmer climates. What are these warmer time periods on Earth known as?

....

Exercise 5.4C Climate cycles

Challenge

This exercise will give you practice in interpreting information from a graph.

The diagram shows the average temperature on Earth over the past 450 000 years. It indicates the time when the Earth was in glacial and interglacial periods.

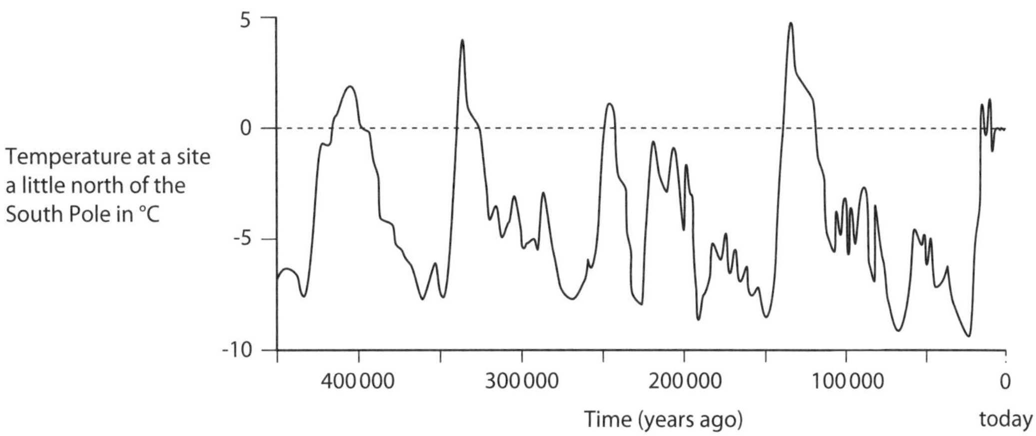

1 Label the glacial and interglacial periods on the graph.

2 How long ago did the last glacial period begin? How long did it last?

....

3 Describe the temperatures in an interglacial period.

....

....

4 What happens to living organisms when the temperatures are well below freezing for a long time?

....

....

5 Describe the pattern of glacial and interglacial periods over the last 450 000 years.

....

....

....

....

....

6 What evidence do we have that the Earth was colder in the past?

....

....

....

5.5 Atmosphere and climate

Exercise 5.5A Our atmosphere

Focus

In this exercise, you will choose words to complete the paragraphs about our atmosphere.

Use the terms here to complete the paragraphs. You may use each term once, more than once or not at all.

Venus fossil fuels locked up carbonates
gases fall carbon rise nitrogen
water vapour carbon dioxide oceans
oxygen photosynthesis atmosphere
volcanoes limestone

In the first billion years after the Earth formed there were lots of

....

These produced ...., which made up the atmosphere.

The .... that was produced condensed, to form lakes

and ....

The early atmosphere was mainly made up of .... gas.

There was little or no .... gas.

This is like the atmosphere of the planet .... today.

As plants began to grow on Earth, they used up the carbon dioxide gas

and produced food by the process of ....

Over billions of years the .... in the carbon dioxide

gas became .... as ...., such as oil

and coal and as .... in sedimentary rocks, such as

....

This caused the levels of carbon dioxide in the atmosphere to

....

Exercise 5.5B Changes in the atmosphere

Practice

In this exercise, you will use information presented on a graph to answer questions.

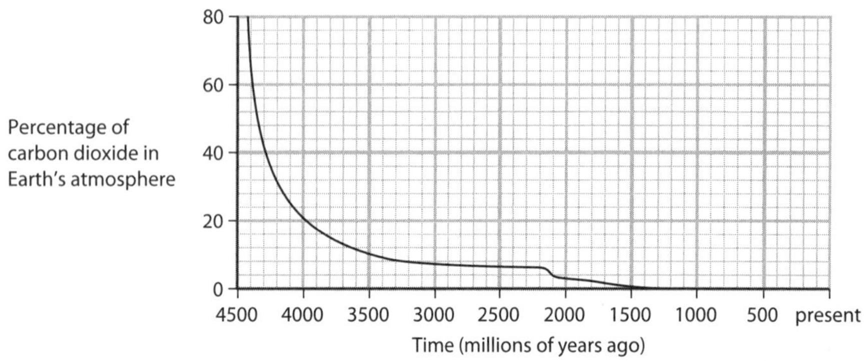

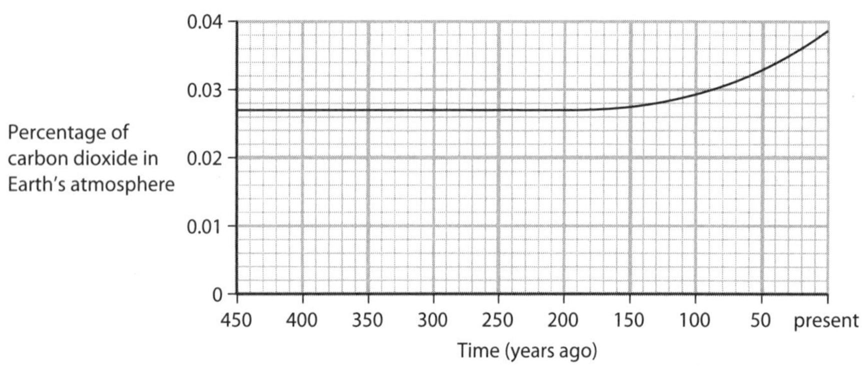

1 What was the percentage of carbon dioxide in the atmosphere 4400 million years ago?

....

2 What was the percentage of carbon dioxide in the atmosphere 3500 million years ago?

....

3 What is the percentage of carbon dioxide in the atmosphere today?

....

4 Describe the changes in the percentage of carbon dioxide in the atmosphere from 4500 to 1500 million years ago.
Explain why that happened.

....

....

....

5 What has happened to the level of carbon dioxide in the atmosphere over the past 200 years?
Why do you think this has happened?

....

....

....

Exercise 5.5C Evidence

Challenge

In this exercise, you will identify the evidence that scientists have for changes in the atmosphere and global warming. You will discuss the reliability of this evidence.

You will need to do some research in order to answer these questions. Make sure you know where the evidence comes from, so that you can decide how reliable the information is.

1 What evidence is there that the atmosphere has changed over time?

....

....

....

....

....

....

....

....

2 What evidence is there to support the idea of global warming?

....

....

....

....

....

....

....

....

....

....

3 Why do you think that the records of the temperatures on Earth taken over the past 100 or so years are more reliable than evidence from earlier times?

....

....

....

....

6 Light

6.1 Reflection

Exercise 6.1A Making reflections

Focus

In this exercise, you will start to describe reflection.

1 Which of these means the same as 'plane mirror'?

Tick (✓) one box.

curved mirror	☐	magnifying mirror	☐
flat mirror	☐	bathroom mirror	☐

2 A moving ball is an analogy for the movement of light. Which of these movements of the ball is an analogy for reflection of light?

Tick (✓) one box.

stopping	☐	bouncing	☐
slowing down	☐	speeding up	☐

3 A ray of light is reflected at a mirror.

Write the name given to:

a the ray of light arriving at a mirror

....

b the ray of light that has been reflected

....

c the line in the ray diagram that is at 90° to the mirror.

....

Exercise 6.1B Ray diagrams

Practice

In this exercise, you will draw ray diagrams for reflection.

1 Complete these ray diagrams.

In each diagram, include:

- the normal
- the reflected ray
- the angle of incidence, *i*
- the angle of reflection, *r*.

You do **not** have to measure any angles.

a

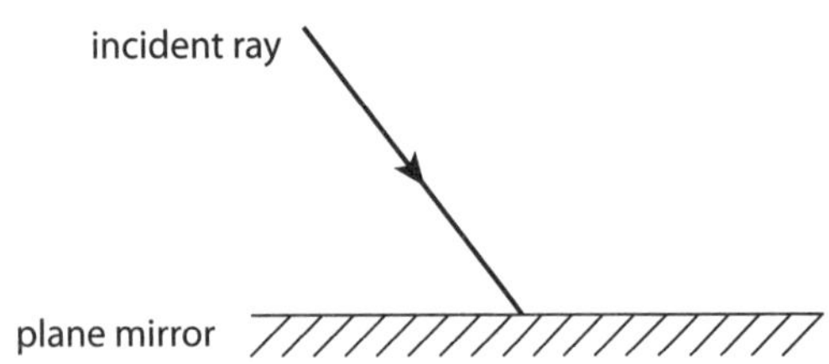

b

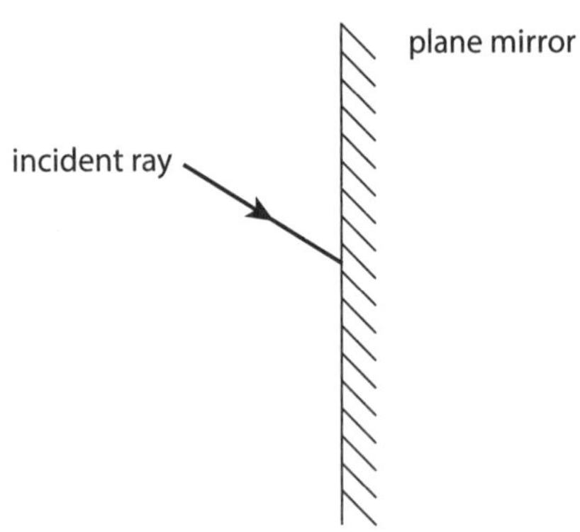

c

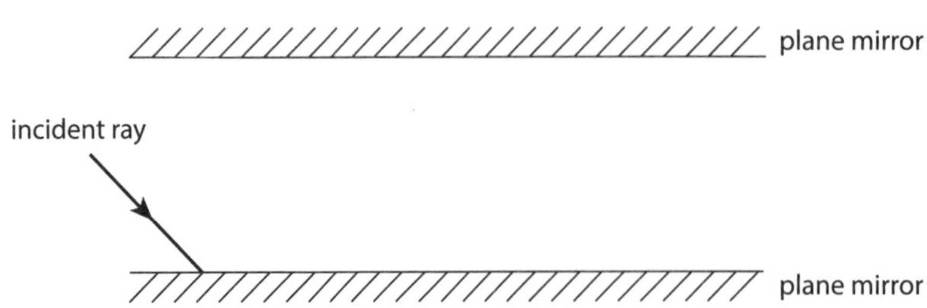

2 **a** Use a protractor or setsquare to draw the normal on this ray diagram.

b Use a protractor to measure the angle of incidence.

angle of incidence

= ....

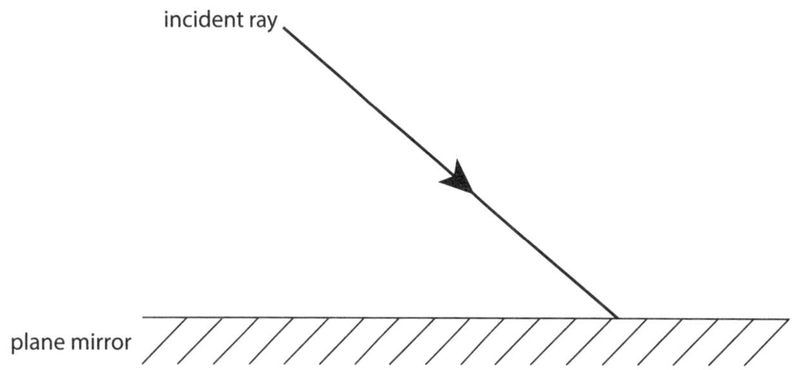

Exercise 6.1C Accurate ray diagrams

Challenge

In this exercise, you will use a protractor to draw accurate ray diagrams.

1 Complete these ray diagrams accurately. Use a protractor.

In each diagram:

- draw the normal accurately
- draw the reflected ray accurately
- write the angle of incidence and the angle of reflection in the correct places.

a

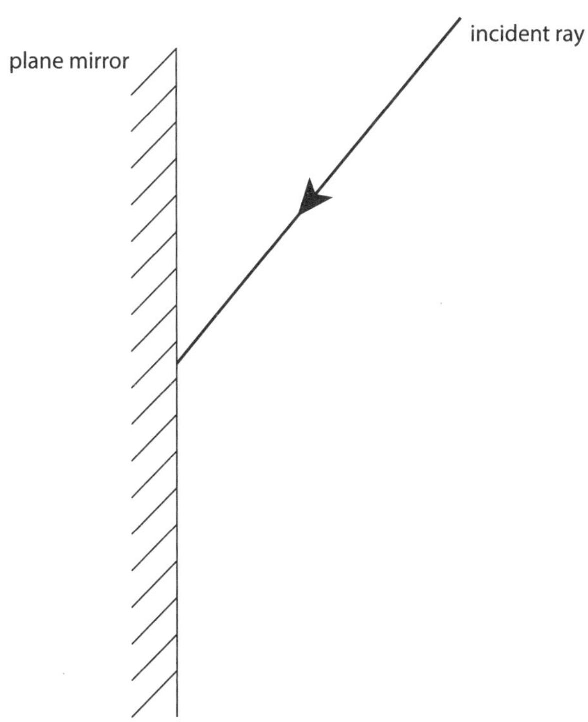

b

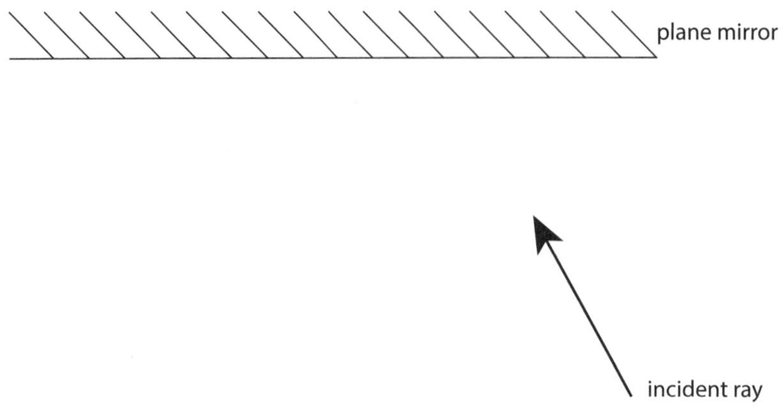

2 Complete this ray diagram accurately.

Show **two** reflections.

Write the angles of incidence and angles of reflection in the spaces below the diagram.

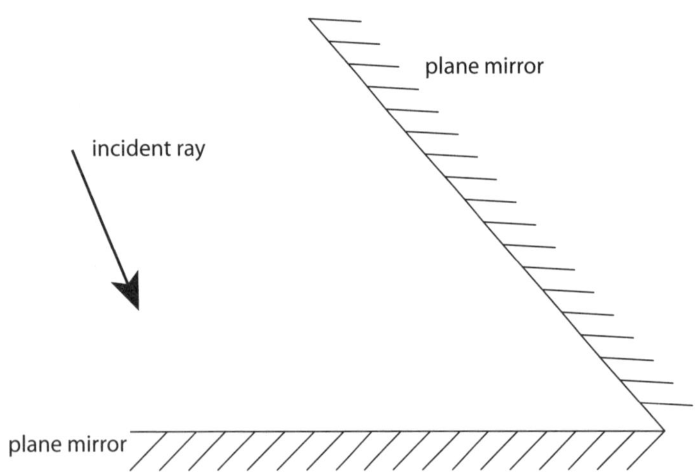

first angle of incidence = ...

first angle of reflection = ...

second angle of incidence = ...

second angle of reflection = ...

6.2 Refraction

Exercise 6.2A Causes of refraction

Focus

In this exercise, you will think about what causes refraction.

1 What name is given to any transparent object that light can pass through?

Choose **one** word from the list.

medium **regular** **normal** **average**

2 The table shows the speed of light in air, in water and in glass.

Transparent substance	Speed of light in km/s
air	300 000
water	225 000
glass	200 000

Use the words **speeds up** or **slows down** to complete these sentences. Use information from the table to help.

a When light passes from air into water, the light ....

b When light passes from glass into air, the light ....

c When light passes from water into glass, the light ....

3 Use words from the list to complete the sentences.

shape **speed** **distance** **refraction** **incident ray** **normal**

When light changes direction, the change in direction can be caused by a change in ....

When light changes direction passing from air into glass, this is called ....

Exercise 6.2B Predicting refraction

Practice

In this exercise, you will predict what happens when light passes between different substances.

1 Explain what causes refraction.

....

....

....

2 The table shows the speed of light in five different transparent substances.

Transparent substance	Speed of light in km/s
air	300 000
water	225 000
corn oil	204 000
glycerol	204 000
diamond	124 000

a In which substance does light travel most slowly?

....

b Between which two substances would there be **most** refraction?

.... and ....

c Between which two substances would there be **no** refraction?

.... and ....

3 Complete these sentences using either the word **towards** or the words **away from**.

When light passes into a medium where it slows down, the light bends .... the normal.

When light passes into a medium where it speeds up, the light bends .... the normal.

4 A window is covered in rain drops.

Explain why you cannot see clearly through the window when it is covered in rain drops.

....

....

....

Exercise 6.2C Refraction ray diagrams

Challenge

In this exercise, you will draw ray diagrams to show how light is refracted.

1 Complete the ray diagrams to show how light is refracted.

Where there are more than two surfaces, show the refraction at each surface.

In each diagram, include:

- the normal
- the angle of incidence, *i*
- the refracted ray
- the angle of refraction, *r*.

You do **not** have to measure any angles.

a

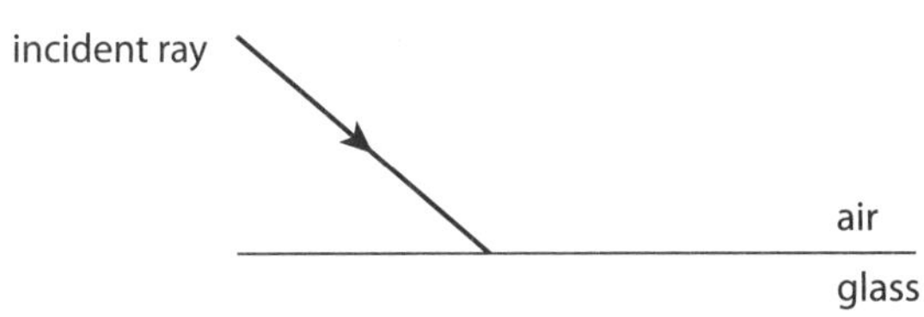

b

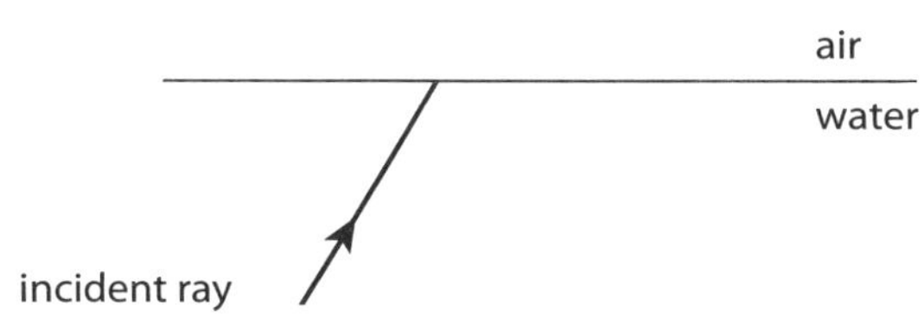

c

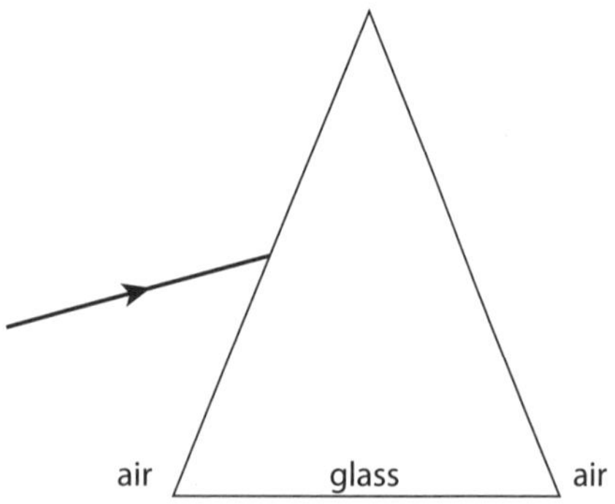

2 Complete the ray diagram to show:

- the normal
- the incident ray.

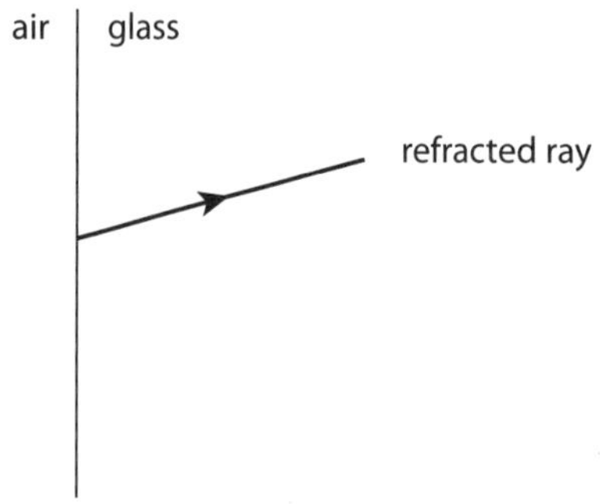

6.3 Making rainbows

Exercise 6.3A Colours of the rainbow

Focus

In this exercise, you will think about the different colours of the rainbow.

1 Which of these describes the range of colours in a rainbow?

Tick (✓) **one** box.

spectrum ☐

section ☐

vacuum ☐

reflection ☐

2 The list shows some of the colours of the rainbow in the correct order.

Complete the list so all the colours are in the correct order.

red, ..., yellow, green, ...,

indigo, ...

3 It is possible to make a rainbow effect in the laboratory by using a prism.

a State the colour of light that needs to shine on the prism to get a complete rainbow effect.

....

b Give the name for splitting this colour of light into the colours of the rainbow.

....

c Which of these describes how the colours appear on a white screen?

Tick (✓) **one** box.

- Each colour is separated from the next one with a white space. ☐
- Each colour is separated from the next one with a black space. ☐
- Each colour merges into the next one with no space. ☐
- Each colour forms a semi-circle around the next one. ☐

Exercise 6.3B Making a spectrum 1

Practice

In this exercise, you will think about how a spectrum of light is formed.

1 The ray diagram shows what happens when white light is separated into the colours of the rainbow, on a screen.

Only four of the colours of the rainbow are labelled.

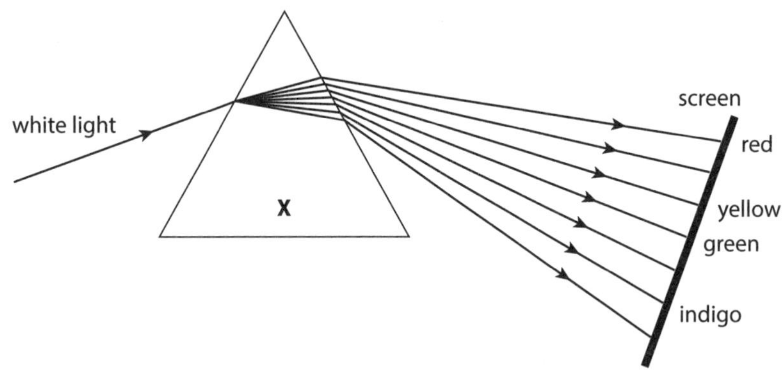

a Name the piece of equipment labelled X in the diagram.

....

b Which colour of light is refracted the most when passing through X?

....

Explain your answer.

....

....

c i State **one** change that would make the colours on the screen brighter. All of the equipment must stay the same.

....

ii State **one other** change in the appearance of the colours when this change is made.

....

Exercise 6.3C Making a spectrum 2

Challenge

In this exercise, you will think in more detail about how a spectrum is formed.

1 Look at the ray diagram.

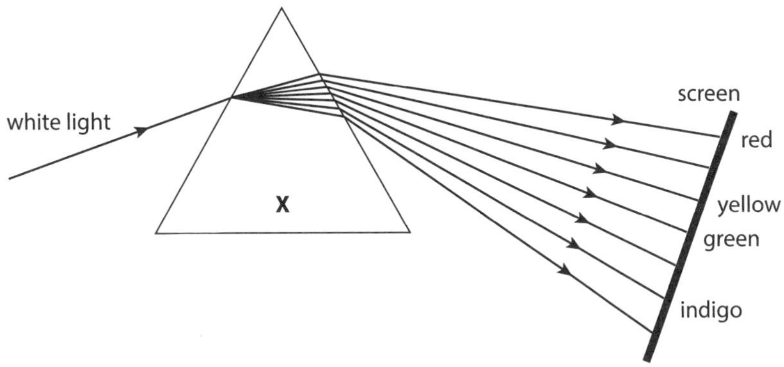

The piece of equipment labelled X is made from a type of transparent plastic.

Use information in the ray diagram to explain how the speeds of the different colours of light compare when passing through this plastic.

....

....

....

....

....

....

....

....

....

6.4 Colours of light

Exercise 6.4A Adding primary colours

Focus

In this exercise, you will think about what happens when colours of light are added.

1 What is meant by the primary colours of light?

Tick (✓) **one** box.

Colours of light that come first in the rainbow. ☐

Colours of light that cannot be made by adding other colours. ☐

Colours of light that can be made by adding any other colours. ☐

Colours of light that are brightest in a rainbow. ☐

2 The primary colours of light are red, green and blue.

Complete the sentences.

a Adding red light and green light makes

.... light.

b Adding green light and blue light makes

.... light.

c Adding red light, green light and blue light makes

.... light.

3 The Sun gives out seven colours of light.

Explain why the light from the Sun appears to be white.

....

....

....

Exercise 6.4B Subtracting colours of light

Practice

In this exercise, you will think about what happens when light passes through coloured filters.

1 White light shines on a red filter.

Green light does **not** pass through the red filter.

a Name **one other** colour of light that does **not** pass through the red filter.

....

b Complete the sentences using words from the list.

transmitted **reflected** **absorbed** **refracted**

The green light has been .... by the red filter.

Red light passes through the filter because red light is

.... by the filter.

2 White light shines on a blue filter.

a State the colour which passes through the blue filter.

....

Explain your answer in terms of subtraction of light.

....

....

....

b The light that passes through the blue filter is made to shine on a green filter.

Explain what will happen.

....

....

3 The sign above a shop gives out yellow light.

The sign uses white lamps.

Explain how white lamps can be used to produce yellow light.

....

....

....

Exercise 6.4C Seeing colours

Challenge

In this exercise, you will think about why objects appear to be different colours.

1 a A green T-shirt appears green in white light.

Use the best words to complete these sentences.

The green T-shirt .... only green light.

The green T-shirt .... all the other colours of light.

b State how the green T-shirt would appear in red light.

....

2 State the colour, or colours, of light that should be used to produce each of these effects.

a Make a red car look red.

.... light or .... light

b Make white paper look blue.

.... light

c Make a green apple appear black.

.... light or .... light

3 a Suggest why scientists do **not** consider black to be a colour.

....

....

b Suggest why scientists do **not** consider white to be a colour.

....

....

6.5 Galaxies

Exercise 6.5A Our own galaxy

Focus

In this exercise, you will think about the galaxy where we live.

1 a Name the galaxy where we live.

....

b Which of these shapes best illustrates the galaxy where we live?

Tick (✓) **one** box.

☐ ☐ ☐

2 a Name the closest star to Earth in our galaxy.

....

b Which of these describes the number of stars in our galaxy?

Tick (✓) **one** box.

fewer than 100 ☐

between 100 and 1000 ☐

between 1000 and 1 000 000 ☐

more than 1 000 000 ☐

3 Write 'true' or 'false' after each of these sentences.

There is a small quantity of dust between the stars in our galaxy.

....

There is a small quantity of gas between the stars in our galaxy.

....

Exercise 6.5B Galaxies in space 1

Practice

In this exercise, you will think about the galaxies that are in space.

1 a Write the word that describes all of space and everything in it.

....

b Explain why we can see other galaxies in space.

....

....

2 Name the three shapes of galaxy.

....

....

....

3 Scientists do **not** know exactly how many galaxies there are in total.

Use the best words to complete these sentences.

Scientists have made an .... of how many galaxies there are in total.

This number may not be ....

Exercise 6.5C Galaxies in space 2

Challenge

In this exercise, you will think in more depth about other galaxies.

1 One type of object in all galaxies is stellar dust.

a List **three other** types of object that must be present in all galaxies.

....

....

....

b Some particles of stellar dust have masses as small as 0.000 000 000 000 001 g.

Suggest how clouds of stellar dust can produce strong forces of gravity in galaxies.

....

....

....

2 a Name the most common type of object that gives out its own light in a galaxy.

....

b Some galaxies contain objects called black holes. A black hole is not actually a hole, but is a solid object.

Suggest **two** reasons why black holes appear black.

1 ....

....

2 ....

....

3 Scientists have discovered that most of the galaxies in space are moving further apart from each other.

Predict **two** ways this will change how other galaxies will be seen from Earth in the future.

1 ....

....

2 ....

....

4 It is possible to estimate the number of grains of sand on a beach.

a Briefly describe how you would do this.

....

....

....

....

b Explain how this is an analogy for estimating the number of galaxies in the Universe.

....

....

....

6.6 Rocks in space

Exercise 6.6A Describing asteroids

Focus

In this exercise, you will describe what asteroids are and where they are found.

1 Which statements describe asteroids?

Tick (✓) **all** that are correct.

All asteroids are larger than planets. ☐

Asteroids are made from rock. ☐

Asteroids can have irregular shapes. ☐

All asteroids orbit the Earth. ☐

2 Where is the asteroid belt?

Tick (✓) **one** box.

Closer to the Sun than Mercury. ☐

Between the orbits of Venus and Earth. ☐

Between the orbits of Mars and Jupiter. ☐

Between the orbits of Uranus and Neptune. ☐

3 State the name given to the path followed by an asteroid around the Sun.

....

Exercise 6.6B Asteroids and planets

Practice

In this exercise, you will describe the differences between asteroids and planets.

1 The Earth has an inner structure consisting of a core, a mantle and a crust.

Most asteroids do **not** have this structure.

List **two** other differences between asteroids and a planet such as Earth.

1 ....

....

2 ....

....

2 All the planets in the Solar System have names.

Suggest **one** reason why **not** all asteroids have names.

....

....

3 The diameter of the asteroid Vesta is $\frac{1}{10}$ of the diameter of the planet Mercury.

Mercury has a diameter of 5000 km.

Calculate the diameter of Vesta.

Show your working.

.... km

Exercise 6.6C Asteroids and planets

Challenge

In this exercise, you will describe the similarities and differences between asteroids and planets and consider the reliability of evidence.

1 List **two** features that asteroids and planets have in common.

1 ....

....

2 ....

....

2 Many planets have one or more moons.

Suggest why most asteroids do **not** have moons.

....

....

3 The total mass of all the asteroids in the asteroid belt is less than any planet.

Explain how this can support the hypothesis that asteroids are rocks left over from the formation of the Solar System.

....

....

....

....

4 The picture shows photographs of some asteroids to show their relative sizes.

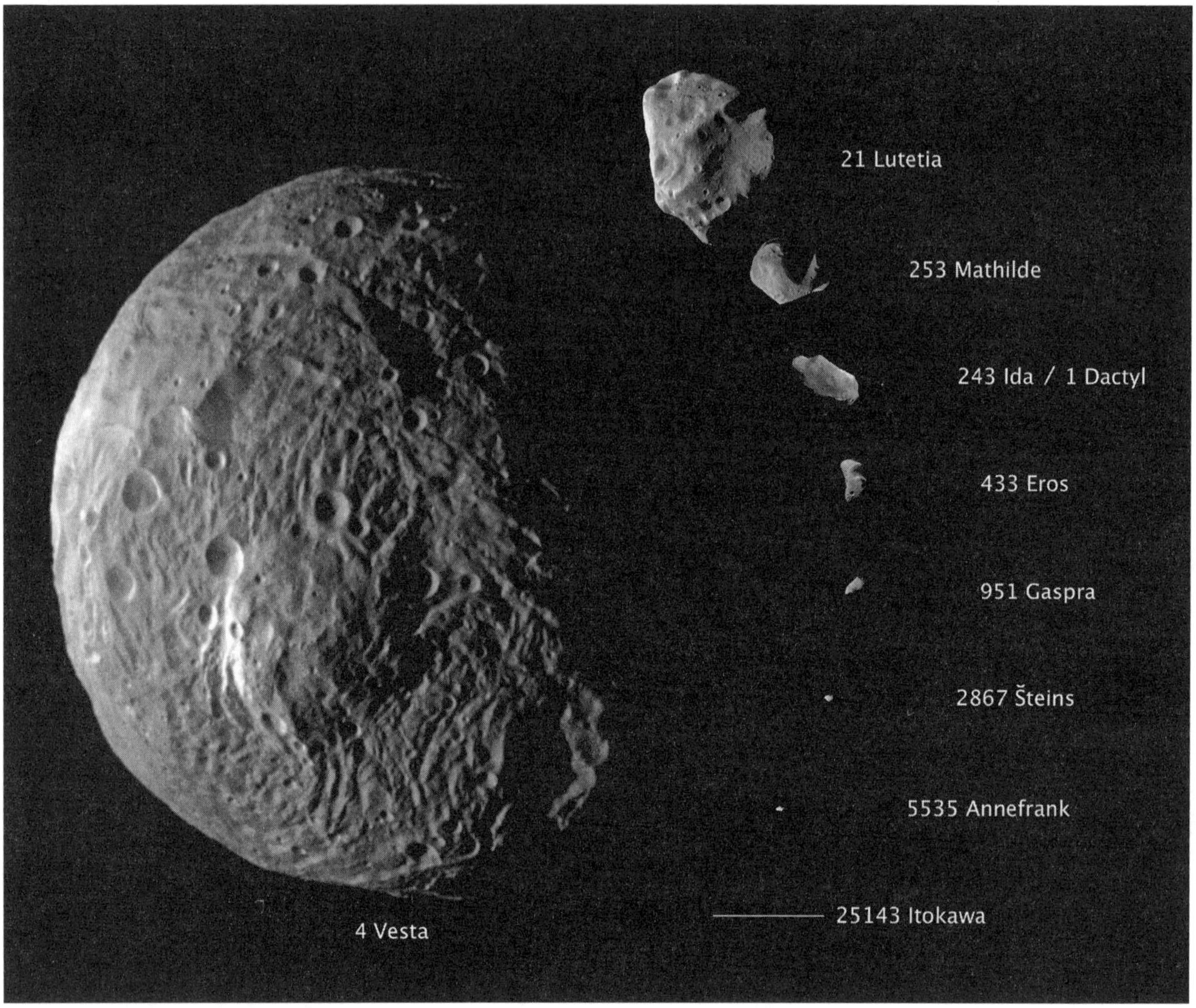

An independent website about aliens claims that a building can be seen on Eros. The website claims that the building was made by aliens. Aliens are forms of life different from those found on Earth.

A university website says that there is no building on Eros. This website says all that can be seen is light reflecting off a crater.

Discuss the reliability of the information in these two websites.

....

....

....

....

....

....

....

7 Diet and growth

7.1 Nutrients

Exercise 7.1A Nutrients and their functions

Focus

In this exercise, you will check that you know the function of each nutrient. Take care – some of the functions might fit two different nutrients, so you will have to choose which one is the better fit.

The first column lists the nutrients that we need in our diet.

The second column lists the functions of the nutrients.

Draw **one** line from each nutrient to its function.

Nutrients	Functions
protein	to make haemoglobin
vitamin A	for growth (making new cells)
calcium	to keep skin strong and able to heal quickly
carbohydrate	for strong bones and teeth
iron	to use in respiration to release energy
vitamin D	to use in respiration to release energy, and to make an energy store under the skin
fat and oil	to help with night vision
vitamin C	to help to absorb calcium, for strong bones and teeth

Exercise 7.1B Analysing information about nutrients

Practice

In this exercise, you will find information from a table to help you to answer the questions.

The table shows some of the nutrients contained in 100 g of different foods.

Food	Protein in g	Fat and oil in g	Carbohydrate in g	Calcium in mg	Vitamin C in mg
brazil nuts	12	60	4	180	0
chapatis	8	13	50	70	0
chicken	29	7	0	0	0
coconut	3	36	4	2	0
fish	18	3	0	0	0
milk	3	4	5	120	1
orange	1	9	9	40	50
tomatoes	1	0	3	0	20

1 Which food contains the most protein?

....

2 Which food contains the most vitamin C?

....

3 How much fat and oil is there in 200 g of milk? (Read the sentence above the table again, before you try to answer this question!)

....

Marcus and Sofia discuss the information in the table.

4 Who is right – Marcus or Sofia?

Explain your answer.

....

....

....

Tip

Look carefully at the headings in the table. There are 1000 mg in 1 g.

5 Which food would be best for a child who has weak teeth and bones? Explain your answer.

Food ....

Explanation

....

....

....

Exercise 7.1C Summarising functions and sources of different nutrients

Challenge

This exercise will help you to bring together information about all of the nutrients, why you need them, and the kinds of foods that supply them.

Complete the table.

Nutrient	Function in the body	Some good sources
protein		meat, fish, pulses
	for energy; as a layer under the skin, it forms an energy store and provides insulation	
carbohydrate		
		green vegetables, carrots, dairy products (foods made from milk)
vitamin C	keeps skin strong	

(continued)

Nutrient	Function in the body	Some good sources
	helps us to absorb calcium	sunlight on skin
calcium		dairy products, seeds
iron		
	a solvent for many different chemicals	any kind of drink

› 7.2 A balanced diet

Exercise 7.2A Fibre in food

Getting started

This exercise asks you to use data given in a table, and to look for a pattern. You will also practise drawing a bar chart.

The table shows the fibre content of some different foods.

Food	Grams of dietary fibre in 100 g of food
apples	2
bananas	3
beans	5
bread, brown	7
bread, white	4
chicken	0
coconut	14
corn	4
eggs	0
fish	0
fries (potato chips)	2
mutton	0
peas	5
plantain	6
potatoes	3
rice	3
spinach	6
sweet potatoes	2
yam	4

1 Explain why we need fibre in our diet.

....

....

2 Look carefully at the table. Which kinds of food do **not** contain any fibre?

....

3 Calculate the total amount of fibre in a meal containing:

200 g of chicken ....

200 g of rice and ....

100 g of spinach ....

total = ...

4 Choose any **ten** of the foods in the table.

Draw a bar chart to show the mass of fibre in 100 g of each food, on the axes provided.

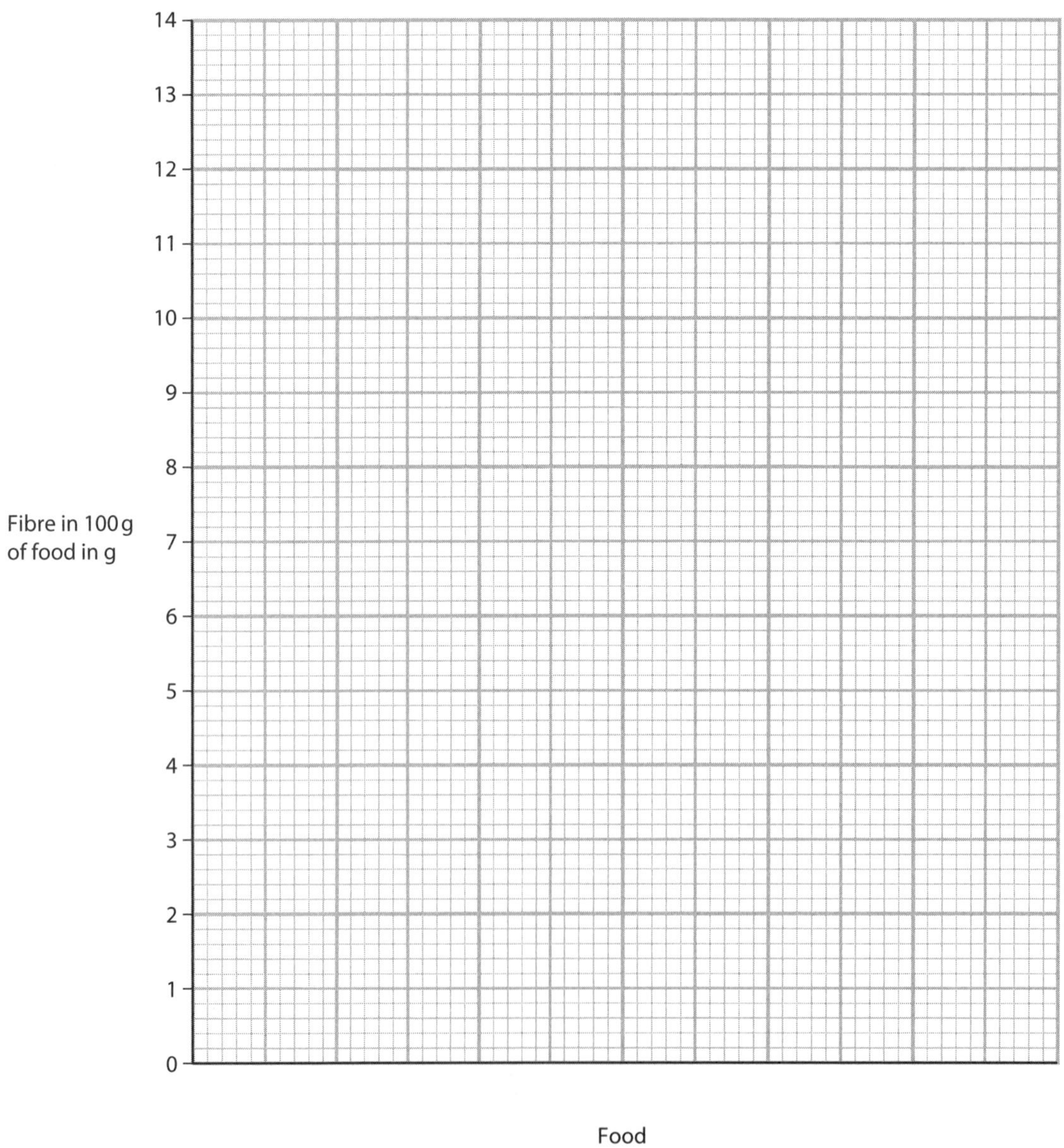

Exercise 7.2B Energy requirements

Practice

In this exercise, you will practise finding information in a written passage and in a bar chart. Make sure that you write the answers in your own words – do not just copy sentences.

Read the information and then answer the questions.

> The cells in your body are always using energy. All of their energy comes from the nutrients in the food that you eat – especially from carbohydrate and fat. Cells can also get energy from protein.
>
> If you eat too much of these nutrients, your cells do not use all of the energy from them. Your body turns the extra nutrients into fat. The fat is stored, mostly just below the skin.
>
> If you don't eat enough of these nutrients to provide all the energy your cells need, the cells have to find another source of energy. They break down the body's fat stores to provide energy. You lose weight.
>
> Different people need different amounts of energy each day. In general, men use more energy than women. People who have active lives use more energy than people who spend a lot of time sitting down.

1 Which **two** nutrients provide most of the energy for the cells in the body?

....

2 A man regularly eats food containing more energy than he uses up each day. What will happen to his weight? Explain your answer.

....

....

3 The bar chart shows the mean energy needs of six different groups of people.

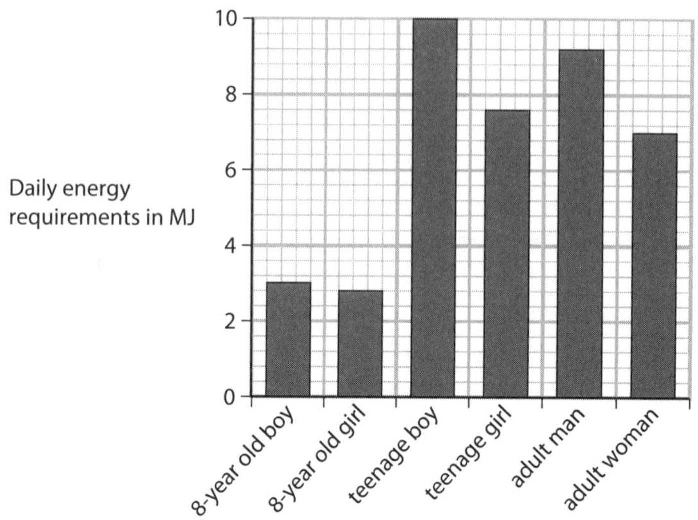

a What are the mean daily energy needs of an eight-year-old girl?

....

b Approximately how much energy should there be in the food that an eight-year-old girl eats each day?

....

c Suggest why an eight-year-old boy needs less energy each day than a teenage boy.

....

....

....

....

d Suggest why, on average, an adult woman needs less energy each day than an adult man does.

....

....

....

....

Exercise 7.2C Planning a diet

Challenge

You are going to plan the meals for one day for your younger sister or brother. The challenge is to make the meals really interesting and tasty, so she or he wants to eat them!

Plan a diet, for one day, for an eight-year-old girl or boy.

Make sure the diet contains some of all of the nutrients.

Explain which nutrients each food contains.

....

....

....

....

....

....

....

....

....

....

....

....

....

....

....

....

....

....

....

....

7.3 Growth, development and health

Exercise 7.3A Interpreting data about smoking

Focus

In this exercise, you will find information in a bar chart. You will use the information to answer questions about how smoking cigarettes affects a person's risk of dying.

The bar chart shows information about people who died from four types of disease in a European country.

The bars show the deaths caused by smoking cigarettes, as a percentage of all deaths from that disease.

There are separate bars for men and women.

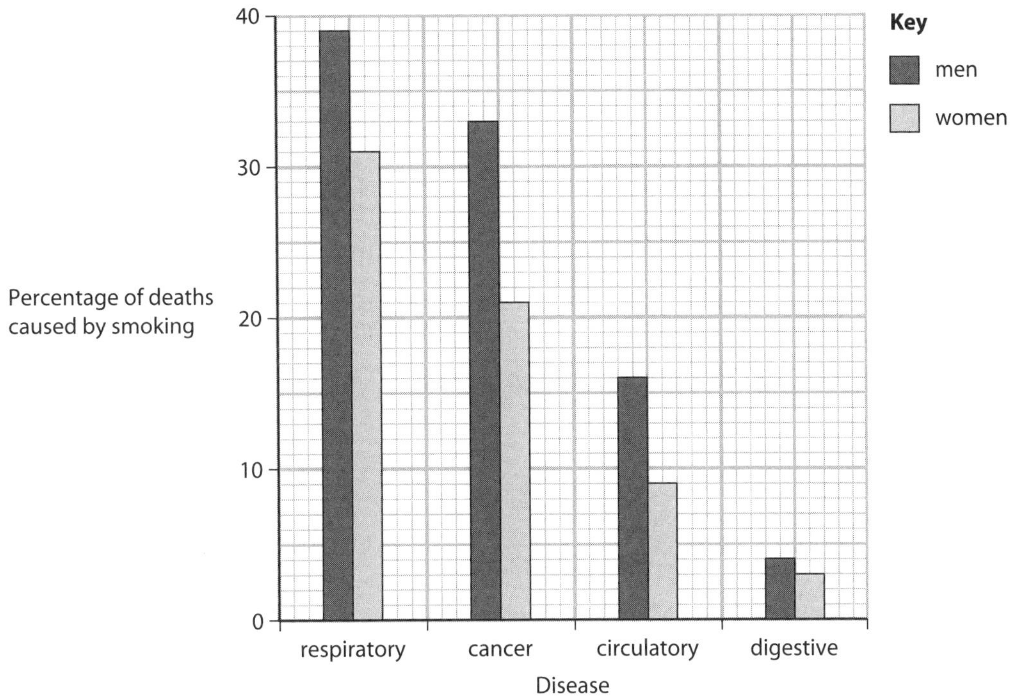

1 For which type of disease can you say:

a death was **most** likely to be caused by smoking?

....

b death was **least** likely to be caused by smoking?

....

2 What percentage of deaths from respiratory disease in men was caused by smoking?

....

3 For every 200 men who died from respiratory disease, how many deaths were caused by smoking?

....

4 What percentage of deaths from cancer in women was caused by smoking?

....

5 For every 500 women who died from cancer, how many deaths were caused by smoking?

....

6 Look at the percentages of deaths caused by smoking for men and women, shown by the whole bar chart.

Draw a circle around **three** words to make this sentence correct.

The bar chart shows that the percentages of deaths due to smoking were (**greater / smaller**) for (**men / women**) than for (**men / women**).

7 Suggest an explanation for the difference stated in question **6**.

....

....

....

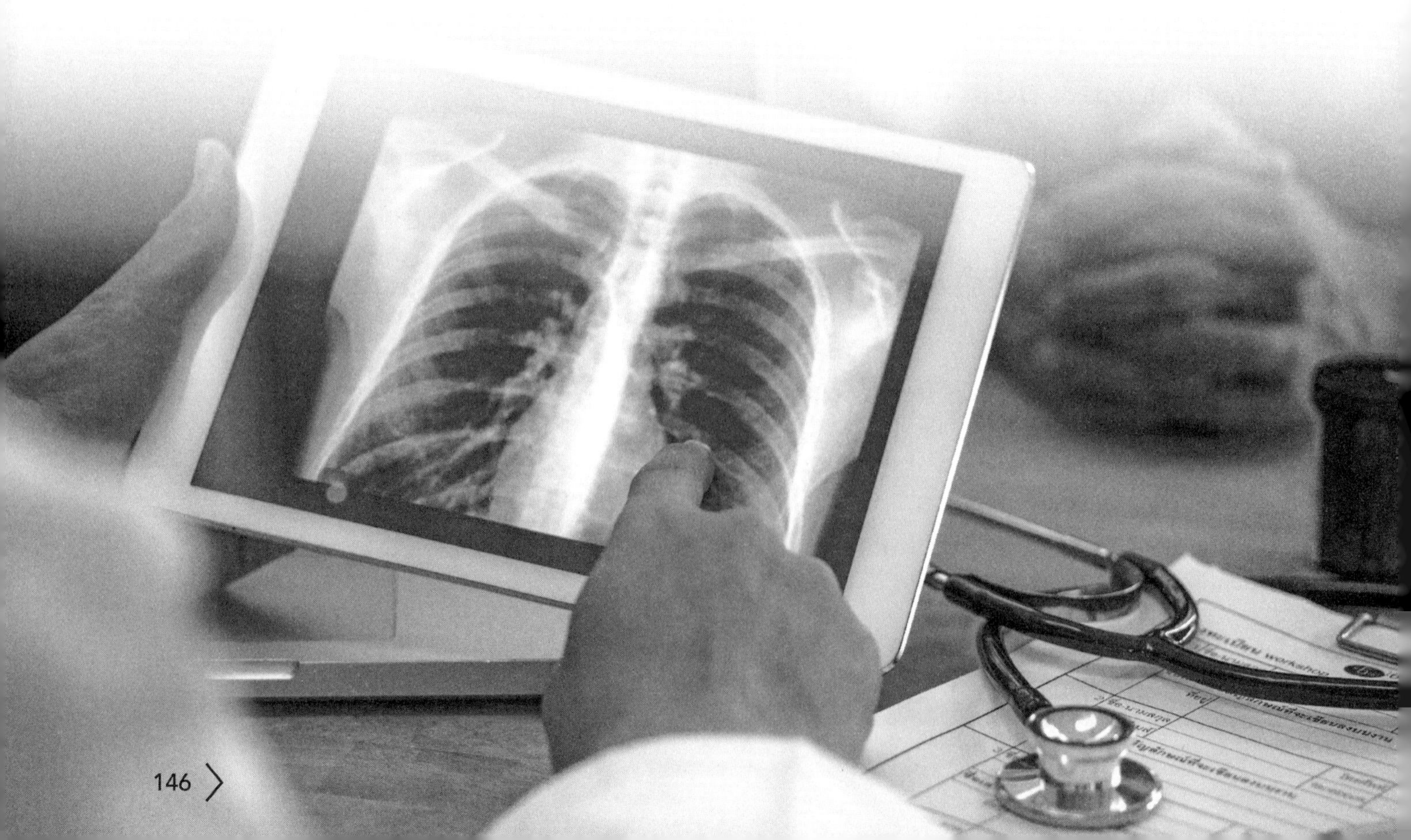

Exercise 7.3B Smoking statistics

Practice

In this exercise, you will practise displaying data in a bar chart. First, though, you will try to find some data yourself, by searching the internet. After you have drawn your bar chart, you will use it to help to answer questions.

The table shows the results of surveys made in nine countries during 2016. They show the percentages of adult women and adult men who were smokers.

Country	Percentage of women who were smokers	Percentage of men who were smokers
Russian Federation	17	45
Chile	31	37
Indonesia	2	65
Netherlands	23	24
Maldives	9	54
Egypt	1	46
Pakistan	2	22
India	3	24
Nigeria	1	10

1 If your country is not listed in the table, use the internet to find the data for it. A good place to look is on the World Health Organization website, and then search for 'tobacco global report'.

If your country is listed, find data for another country that you are interested in.

Country ....

Percentage of women who were smokers: ....

Percentage of men who were smokers: ....

2 On the grid provided, construct a bar chart to display the data in the table, and the other data that you have found.

3 a In which country did the greatest percentage of women smoke in 2016?

....

b In which country did the greatest percentage of men smoke in 2016?

....

c In which country was there the biggest difference in the percentage of women who smoked, and the percentage of men who smoked?

....

Exercise 7.3C Looking at data on giving up smoking

Challenge

In this challenging task, you will practise finding information in text. You will select some of this information to construct a results chart and draw a graph. Lastly, you will combine information from different sources to assist you to make a suggestion.

In 2003, a survey was carried out in China to investigate how many smokers had given up smoking or wanted to give up smoking.

The survey found that 2.5% of men who had been smokers and 3.2% of women who had been smokers had successfully given up. Another 3.6% of the men and 3.9% of the women were trying to give up smoking.

The people who had been successful in giving up smoking were asked why they had given up: 41% said that it was because they had become ill; 27% said it was because they were worried that they might become ill; 12% had given up because of the cost of cigarettes; 5% had given up because their families disapproved of them smoking; 5% had given up because their doctor had told them to. The remainder had a mixture of different reasons for giving up.

The survey also collected data about people who had tried to give up smoking but had failed. 54% of these people said they had gone back to smoking because they could not manage without cigarettes. 4% said their health had improved, so they thought it would be OK to start smoking again. 39% explained that it was difficult not to smoke when everyone else around them was smoking. The remaining 12% had other reasons for failing to give up smoking.

1 When you have read the whole text carefully, choose **one** set of survey results that you can use to construct a results table and graph.

Write down what your chosen set of results is about.

....

....

2 Construct a results table and fill in your chosen results.

3 Display your data in the best way you can. For example, you could use a pie chart in the space below or a bar graph on the grid provided.

4 Since the survey was carried out, electronic cigarettes (e-cigarettes) have become available. These provide the smoker with nicotine, but are less likely to make the smoker ill.

Using the information from the survey, and your own knowledge of the effects of nicotine, suggest how e-cigarettes might help more people to give up smoking.

....

....

....

....

7.4 Moving the body

Exercise 7.4A The skeleton and forces

Focus

In this exercise, you will practise reading and completing a results table.

Arun does an experiment to measure how much force he can produce with the muscles in his fingers.

He hooks a forcemeter to the bench.

Then he pulls the forcemeter with the index finger of his right hand.

Here is a close-up of the scale on the forcemeter.

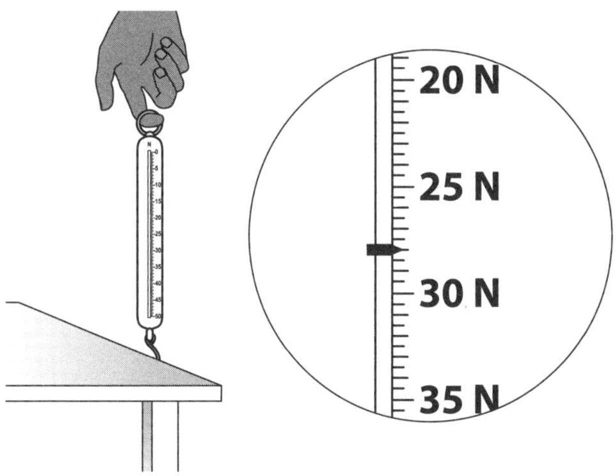

1 Who reads the scale correctly?

Tick (✓) the box under the correct reading.

Arun now pulls the forcemeter with the thumb of his right hand, and then with his other three fingers.

These pictures show the forcemeter scale for each.

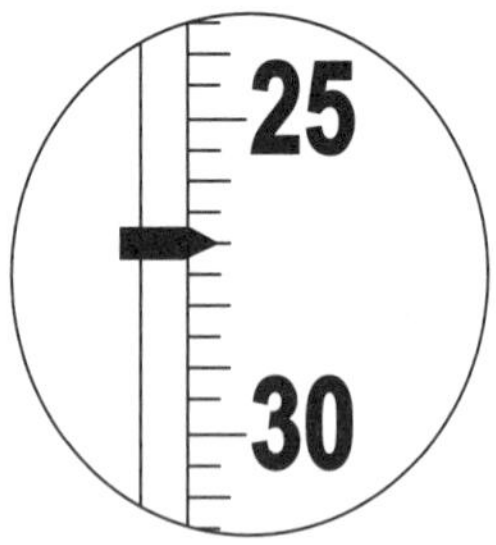

thumb

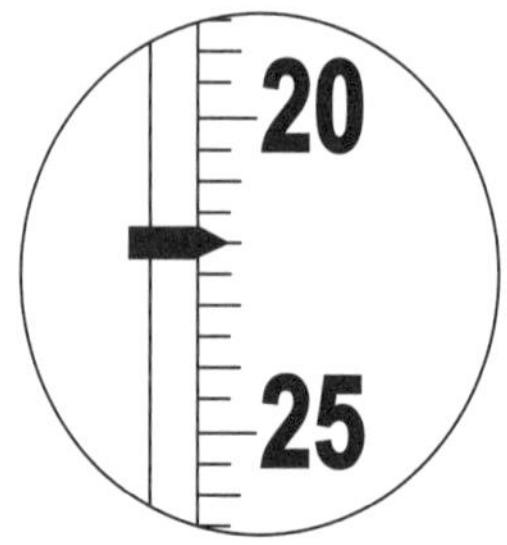

second finger

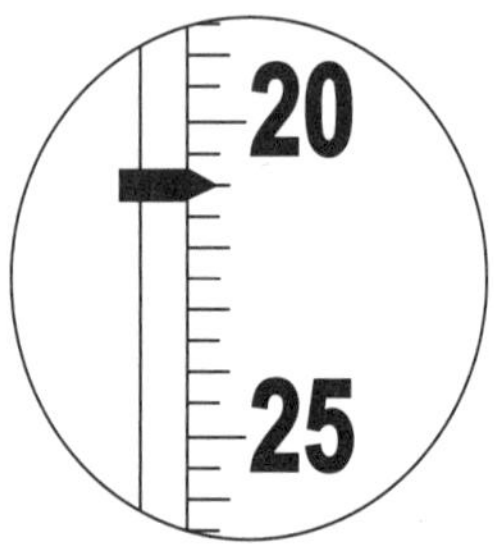

third finger

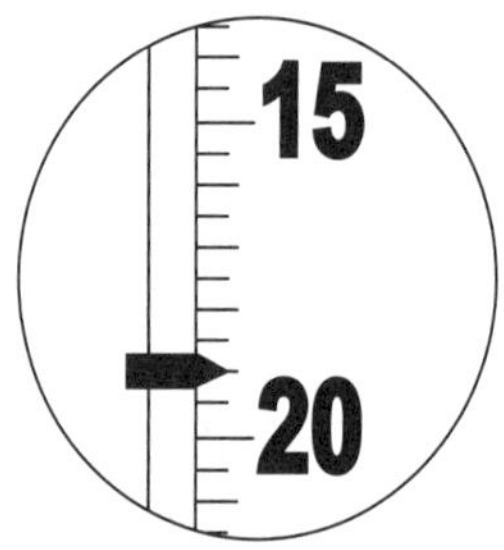

little finger

Write the readings in the correct spaces in the results table.

The readings for Arun's left hand are already completed.

	Force in N	
	Right hand	Left hand
thumb		25
first finger		25
second finger		19
third finger		16
little finger		17

Exercise 7.4B Antagonistic muscles in the leg

Practice

In this exercise, you will use what you have learnt about the muscles in the arm to predict how the muscles in the leg work.

The diagram shows the muscles in a person's leg.

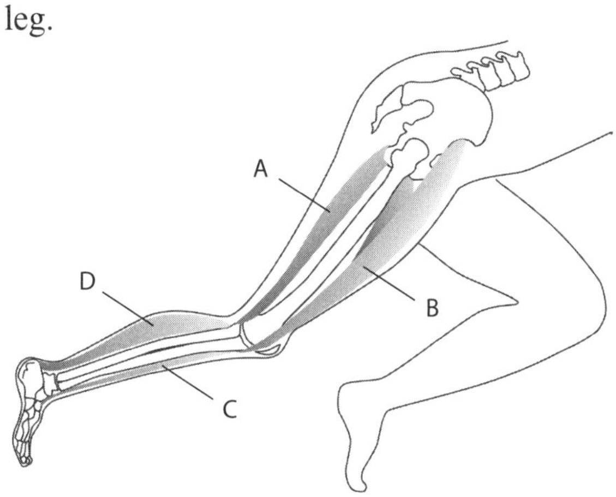

1 On the diagram, label these bones. You can use the picture of the skeleton in the Learner's Book to help you.

femur **pelvis** **tibia**

2 What kind of joint is the knee joint?

....

3 On the diagram, label a ball-and-socket joint.

4 Look carefully at the diagram. What will happen at the knee joint when muscle **A** contracts?

....

5 What will happen at the knee joint when muscle **B** contracts?

....

6 Which of these pairs of muscles are antagonistic pairs? Underline the **two** correct answers.

A and **B** **A** and **D** **B** and **B** **C** and **D** **C** and **A**

Exercise 7.4C Choosing a hypothesis about bones to investigate

Challenge

In this task, you will choose a hypothesis that can be tested by experiment. Then you will plan an experiment to test the hypothesis, and think about how your results could support or contradict the hypothesis.

The diagram shows apparatus that can be used to measure the force needed to make a paper drinking straw break.

You can use the drinking straw to represent a leg bone or arm bone.

To do the experiment, pull gently and steadily on the forcemeter until the straw suddenly bends.

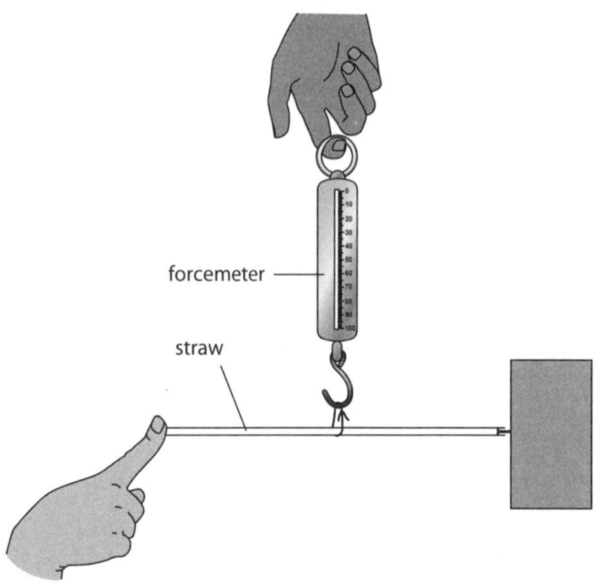

1 Here are four hypotheses about bones. Tick (✓) the **two** hypotheses that could be tested using a method similar to the one shown in the diagram.

Thick bones are stronger than thin bones.	☐
People who eat plenty of calcium have stronger bones than people who do not.	☐
Old bones break more easily than young bones.	☐
Long bones break more easily than short bones.	☐

2 Choose **one** of the hypotheses that you have ticked in question **1**.

Write the hypothesis here.

....

....

Plan an experiment to test your chosen hypothesis. Your experiment should use a method similar to the one shown in the diagram.

a What will you change in your experiment?

....

b What will you measure to collect your results?

....

c Which variables will you try to keep the same?

....

....

....

d Describe clearly how you will do your experiment.

....

....

....

....

....

....

....

....

....

....

e Describe any risks in your experiment, and how you will control them.

....

....

....

f Draw a results chart that you could use. Include headings and units.

g Predict the results that you expect you will get. Explain your prediction.

....

....

....

....

8 Chemical reactions

> 8.1 Exothermic reactions

Exercise 8.1A Investigating an exothermic reaction

Focus

In this exercise, you will identify variables and interpret results.

Sofia and Marcus are measuring the temperature rise in a reaction between magnesium ribbon and hydrochloric acid.

They want to find out if using a longer piece of magnesium ribbon makes the temperature rise higher.

1 What is the independent variable in this investigation?

....

2 What is the dependent variable? ....

3 What are the control variables? State at least two.

....

....

Sofia and Marcus do some tests first, to find out how much they must change the length of magnesium each time. This change in the variable is called the **interval**.

4 Here are the results of these tests. Complete the table.

Length of ribbon in cm	Start temperature in °C	End temperature in °C	Temperature change in °C
0.5	19.0	36.0	
1.0	19.0	36.0	
1.5	19.0	36.5	

5 Describe what the results show.

....

....

6 Do Sofia and Marcus have enough data to say that their prediction is correct? ....

Explain your answer.

....

....

7 What is the interval in length they used? ....

8 Should they use a larger or smaller interval for the main investigation? ....

Explain why.

....

....

9 Suggest how many different lengths of magnesium ribbon they should use. ....

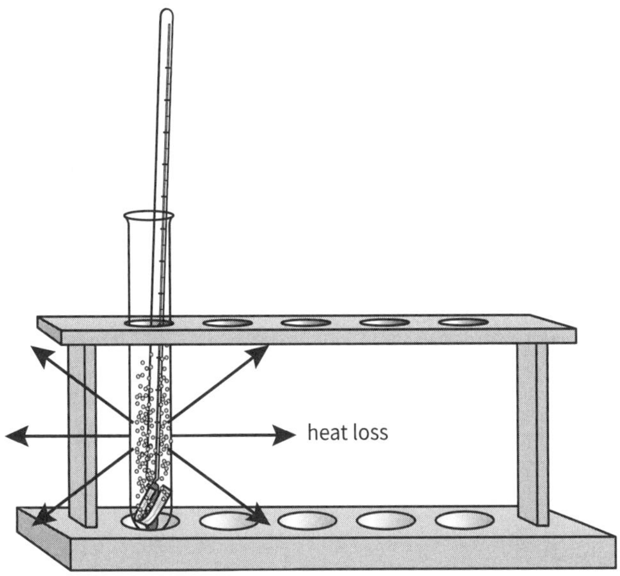

10 How can Sofia and Marcus reduce the heat loss from the test tube?

....

11 Explain how they can make sure their results are reliable.

....

....

Exercise 8.1B Investigating exothermic reactions between metals and acid

Practice

This exercise you will help you to look critically at the evidence from an investigation.

1 Write a word equation for the reaction between magnesium and sulfuric acid.

....

2 Zara and Arun are carrying out an investigation to find out which of the metals X or Y produces the higher temperature in a reaction with hydrochloric acid.

Zara measures out 10 cm^3 of hydrochloric acid in a test tube. She measures the temperature and then places a small piece of metal X into the acid. She sees bubbles of gas given off. When the reaction finishes, she measures the temperature again.

Arun measures out 10 cm^3 of hydrochloric acid in a test tube. He measures the temperature and then places a piece of metal Y into the acid. He also sees bubbles of gas given off. When the reaction finishes, he measures the temperature again.

Zara's experiment

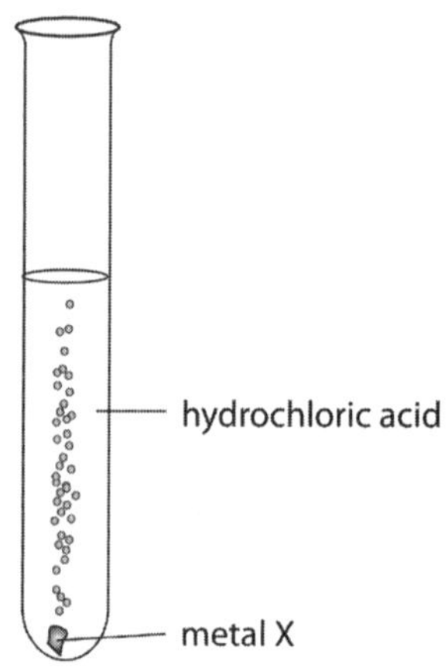

Arun's experiment

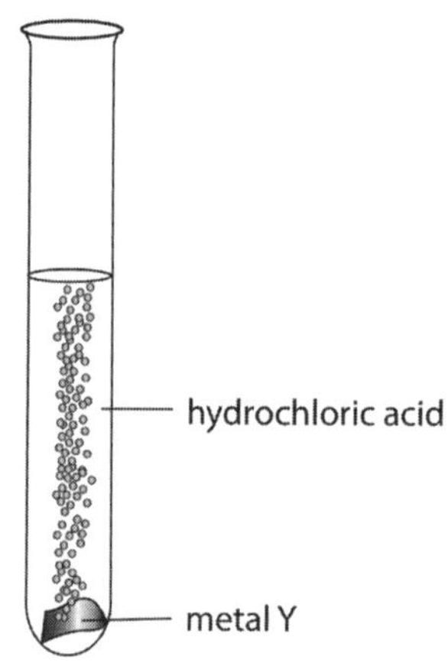

The diagrams show the test tubes **just** after the metals have been added.

a Which variable did Zara and Arun need to change in their investigation?

....

b Which variable or variables have they kept the same?

....

c There is one variable that Zara and Arun changed, but which they should have kept the same. What is this variable?

....

d In the reaction with metal X, the temperature increased by 2°C. In the reaction with metal Y the temperature increased by 6°C.

What conclusions can you draw from these results?

....

....

e Suggest how Zara and Arun could improve their investigation and make their results more reliable.

....

....

Exercise 8.1C Exothermic reactions with metals

Challenge

In this exercise, you will answer questions about exothermic reactions. Then you will plan an investigation and suggest how to present some results.

When potassium reacts with water, energy is changed from chemical energy.

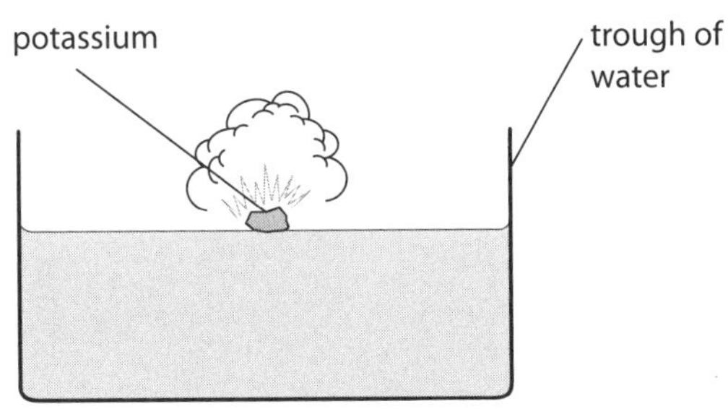

1 Write the word equation for this reaction.

....

2 What is the chemical energy changed to in this reaction?

....

....

3 What safety precautions should be taken when this reaction is carried out?

....

....

4 Suggest a way of measuring the energy given out in this reaction.

....

....

....

5 Explain how you would carry out an investigation to answer the question:

Do different metals produce different increases in temperature when they react with acid?

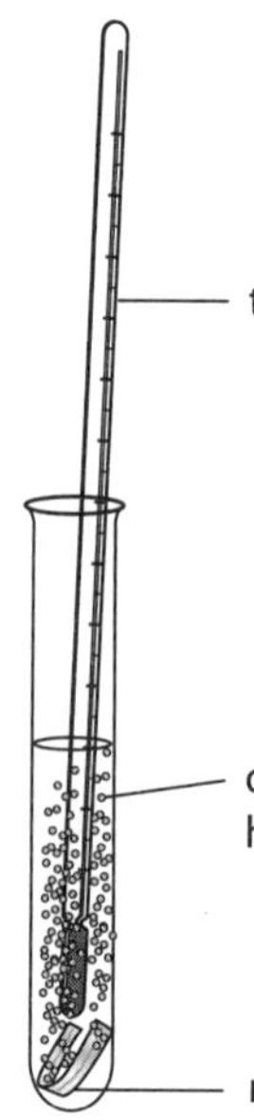

....

....

....

....

....

....

....

....

....

....

....

....

....

....

....

....

6 Amal investigates the question above using four metals in hydrochloric acid. These are his results.

Metal	Rise in temperature in °C
A	10
B	11
C	14
D	4

Which type of graph would you suggest Amal use to present these results?

....

Give a reason for your choice.

....

....

....

....

› 8.2 Endothermic reactions

Exercise 8.2A Energy changes

Focus

In this exercise, you will complete a table and decide if reactions are exothermic or endothermic.

> **Remember:** In an **exothermic reaction** energy is transferred **to** the surroundings and the temperature **increases.** In an **endothermic reaction** energy is transferred **from** the surroundings and the temperature **decreases.**

1 For each of the reactions in the table, write **exothermic** or **endothermic.**

Reaction	Start temperature in °C	Final temperature in °C	Exothermic or endothermic
A	21	45	
B	18	22	
C	19	16	
D	18	20	

2 Sherbet sweets react in your mouth to give a cool, fizzy feeling. Is this an exothermic or endothermic reaction?

....

3 When magnesium ribbon reacts with hydrochloric acid, the testtube gets warm. Is this an exothermic or endothermic reaction?

....

Exercise 8.2B Exothermic or endothermic?

Practice

In this exercise, you will use data to distinguish between exothermic and endothermic reactions and answer some questions.

1 Sofia and Marcus have investigated various reactions to find out if they are exothermic or endothermic. The bar chart below shows their results.

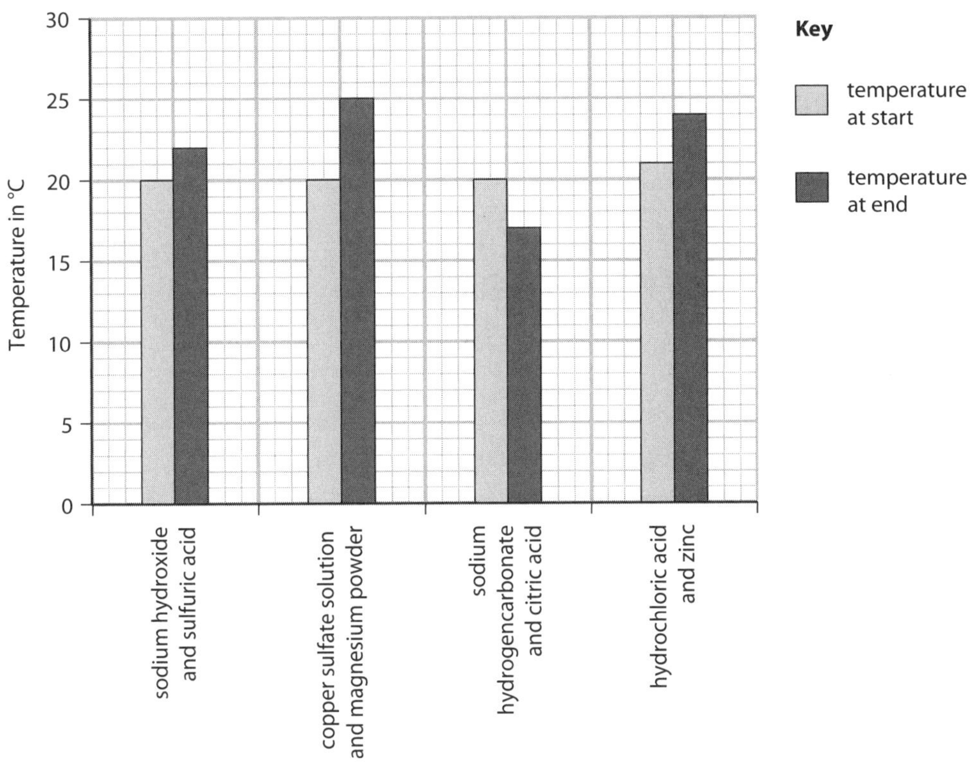

a Which of the reactions are endothermic and which exothermic?

....

....

....

....

b Which of these reactions has the largest temperature change?

....

c Sofia and Marcus used insulated cups rather than test tubes or glass beakers for their reactions. Suggest why this was a sensible idea.

....

....

2 Give an example of a useful product that involves an exothermic reaction or process.

....

3 Give an example of a useful product that involves an endothermic reaction or process.

....

Exercise 8.2C Endothermic reactions and processes

Challenge

In this exercise, you will explain the difference between an endothermic reaction and an endothermic process and describe, using particle theory what happens during one of these processes.

1 Explain the difference between an endothermic **reaction** and an endothermic **process**.

Give **one** example of each.

....

....

....

....

....

....

2 Arun and Marcus are camping in a tent during a spell of hot weather. They have no refrigerator to keep their drinks cool. They place their bottles of soda in a bowl with water, and place a wet cloth over the top.

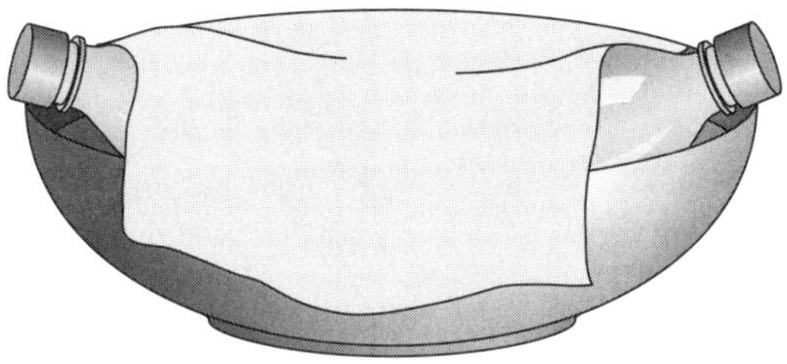

Use particle theory to help you explain why this arrangement will help to keep their bottles of soda cool.

....

....

....

....

....

....

› 8.3 Reactions of metals with oxygen

Exercise 8.3 Why does iron rust?

In this exercise, you will practise using what you know about iron rusting.

Focus

Rusting is a chemical reaction that is not useful. Zara is investigating the conditions needed to make iron nails rust. She has set up the experiment shown in the following diagram.

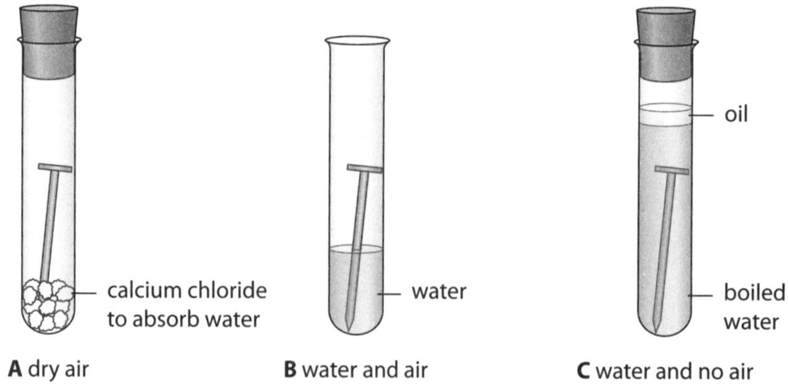

1 What is the chemical name for rust?

....

2 In which tube will the nail go rusty?

....

3 How do the conditions in tube C prevent air reaching the iron nail?

....

....

Practice

4 In Zara's experiment, she notices that the nail in tube A goes a little rusty.

a Is this an expected result? ....

b Suggest how this nail could have rusted.

....

....

5 What could be done to the iron nails to stop them from rusting? Suggest **two** ideas.

....

....

Challenge

6 Plan an investigation to find out if an iron nail rusts more quickly when it is warm rather than cold.

Remember to think about the variable you will change, the variables you will keep the same and the variable you will measure.

....

....

....

....

....

....

....

....

....

....

....

....

....

....

....

....

....

....

8.4 Reactions of metals with water

Exercise 8.4 Reactions with water and steam

In this exercise, you will practise writing word equations. It will also help you to think about the reactions with water and steam.

Focus

The table summarises the reactions of some metals with water.

Metal	Reaction with water
zinc	reacts only with steam
copper	no reaction
potassium	the metal bursts into flames
magnesium	slow reaction with water

1 Place the metals in order of their reactivity with water. Start with the most reactive.

Most reactive	
Least reactive	

2 Write the word equation for the reaction between potassium and water.

....

3 Name another metal that reacts in a similar way to potassium.

....

Practice

4 Using the information above, explain why copper is used for the roofs of some buildings and magnesium is not.

....

....

5 Write the word equation for the reaction between calcium and water.

....

6 This apparatus was set up to demonstrate the reaction of some metals with steam. Label the diagram.

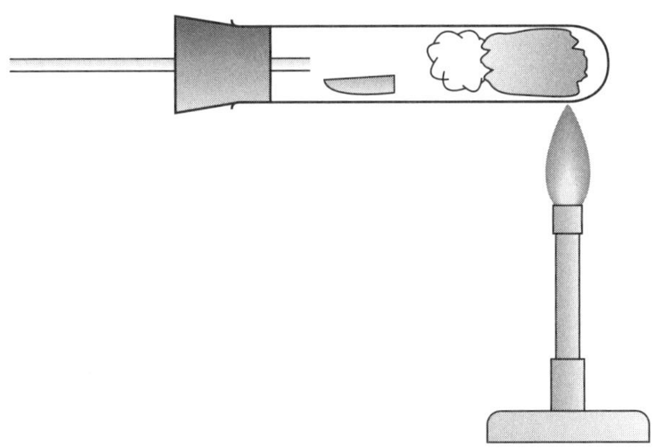

7 Which gas is given off in this reaction?

....

8 How do you test for this gas?

....

9 Write the word equation for the reaction between magnesium and steam.

....

Challenge

10 A metal, such as magnesium or calcium, reacts with water. Draw and label the apparatus you could use to collect the gas given off in this reaction.

11 Copper pipes are used to carry water and in heating systems. Explain why copper is used and explain what would happen if pipes made of iron were used.

....

....

....

....

8.5 Reactions of metals with dilute acids

Exercise 8.5A Investigating reactivity

Focus

In this exercise, you will practise identifying variables in an investigation.

Arun and Marcus are investigating the reaction of different metals with acid.

They have four metals, **A**, **B**, **C**, and **D**, and they want to compare how reactive these are.

They place a piece of each of the metals into a test tube of dilute hydrochloric acid. They watch to see how many bubbles it produces.

1 The result for one metal from the test cannot be compared with the others. Explain why.

....

....

2 What have Arun and Marcus done to keep safe?

....

Two other pairs of learners do the same investigation.
Sofia and Zara set up the experiment like this.

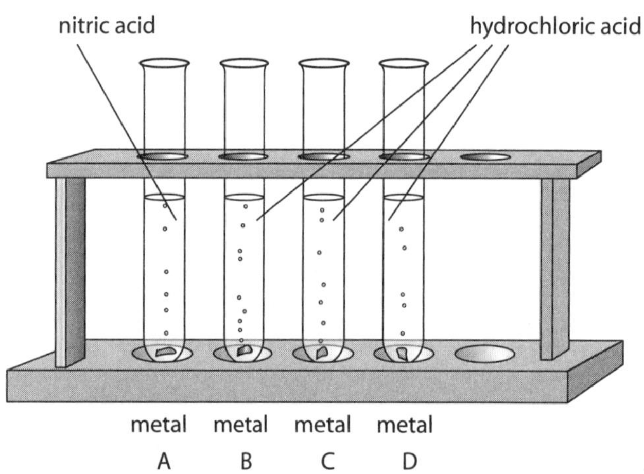

3 Why is Sofia and Zara's test **not** a fair test?

....

....

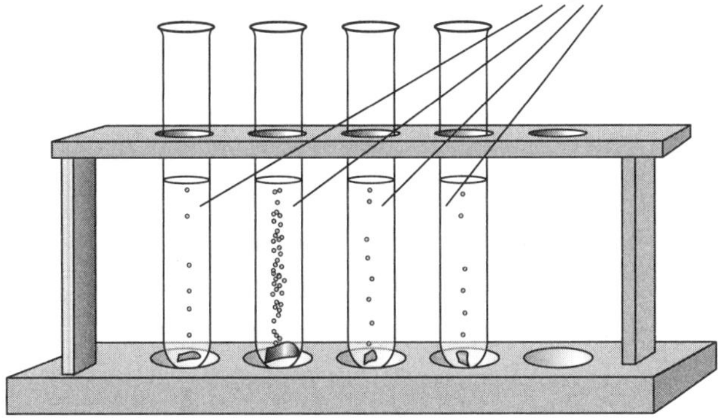

4 This experiment was done by other learners in the class.
Is it a fair test? Explain your answer.

....

....

5 What are they trying to find out in their investigations?

....

....

6 What should they change in the investigation?

....

7 What should they measure or observe in the investigation?

....

8 Which variables should they keep the same in the investigation?
State at least three.

....

....

....

Exercise 8.5B Reactions of metals with dilute acids

Practice

This exercise will give you practice in planning a fair investigation.

Marcus and Arun are carrying out an investigation into the reactivity of different metals with dilute acids. They place a small piece of each metal into a test tube of acid and observe the reaction.

1 How can they tell that a reaction has taken place?

....

2 How can they tell which metal is more reactive?

....

Marcus carries out the test on zinc and lead. Arun carries out the test on copper and aluminium. Marcus uses dilute hydrochloric acid and Arun uses very dilute sulfuric acid for his tests.

Marcus's investigation

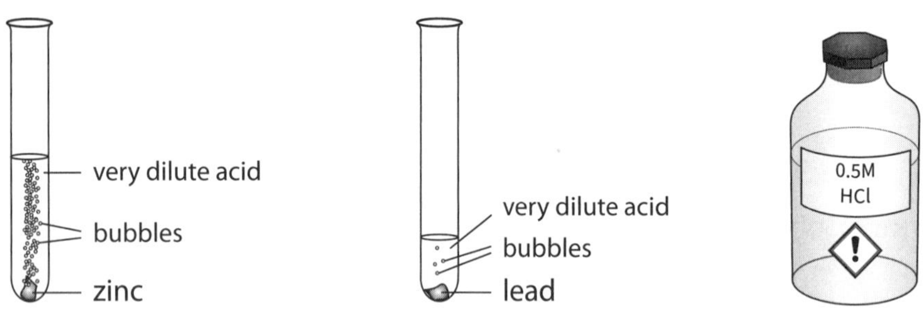

Arun's investigation

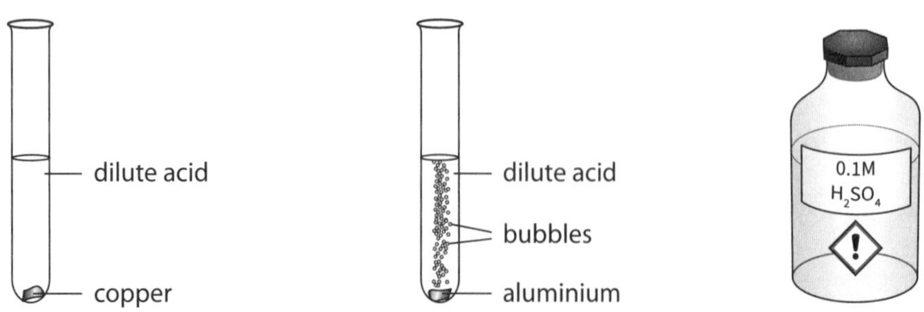

3 Explain why Marcus and Arun cannot use their observations to decide if copper or aluminium are more or less reactive than lead or zinc.

....

....

4 Write a plan for them to carry out this investigation so that their results are more reliable and can be compared fairly.

Remember to include safety information.

....

....

....

....

....

....

....

....

....

....

....

....

....

....

....

....

Exercise 8.5C How reactive are these metals?

Challenge

In this exercise, you will identify variables and practical difficulties in an investigation. You will also present and discuss some results.

Zara is asked to investigate the reactivity of six metals with dilute hydrochloric acid. The metals produce hydrogen when they are added to dilute hydrochloric acid.

The equipment she will use is shown in the diagram.

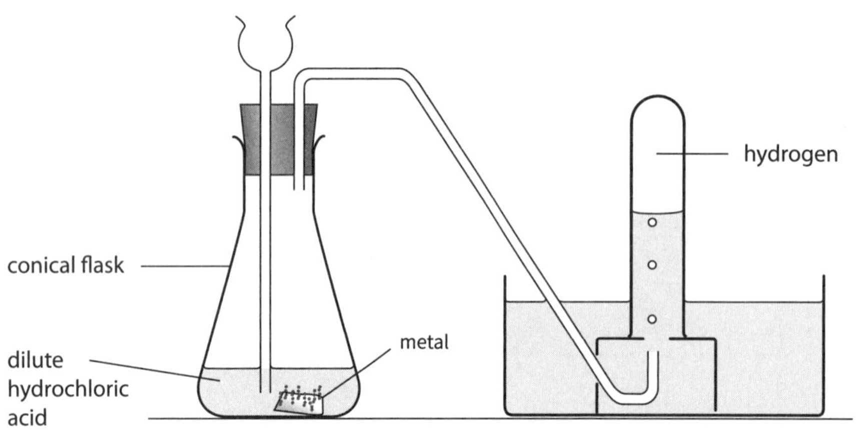

Zara adds a metal to the acid and then times how long it takes to collect a test tube full of hydrogen. The metals she is using are magnesium, zinc, iron, copper, lead and aluminium.

1 Which variables should Zara control in order to ensure the test is fair?

State at least three.

....

....

....

Here are Zara's results.

Metal	Time to collect test tube of hydrogen in s
aluminium	27
zinc	54
magnesium	21
lead	69
iron	49

2 No results for copper are recorded. Suggest why Zara has not included this.

....

....

3 Present these results on the grid supplied. Present them in order with the **least reactive** first.

Zara notices an anomaly in her results. Zinc is only a little less reactive than aluminium, yet the result she has shows that zinc is a lot less reactive than aluminium.

4 Suggest how Zara could have obtained this odd result.

....

....

....

5 Explain the practical difficulties in using this method to obtain accurate results.

....

....

....

....

6 Suggest how Zara could improve the accuracy of her results.

....

....

....

....

9 Magnetism

9.1 Magnetic fields

Exercise 9.1A Magnetic field patterns

Focus

In this exercise, you will start to think about what magnetic fields show.

1 Look at the magnetic field pattern around this magnet.

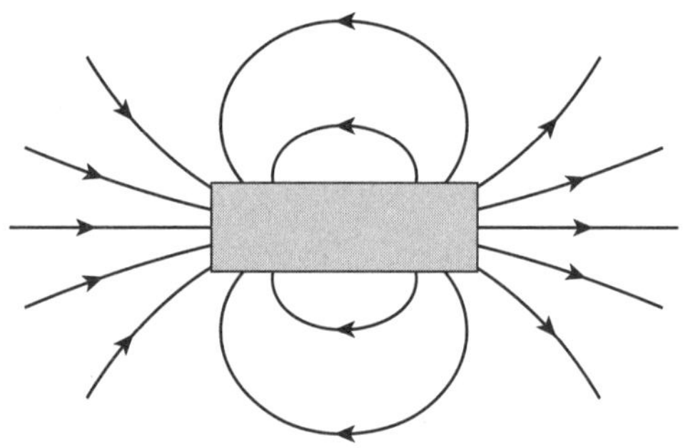

a Write the letters N and S on the diagram to show the poles of the magnet.

b Mark, with the letter X on the diagram, **one** position where the magnetic field is strong.

c Mark, with the letter W on the diagram, **one** position where the magnetic field is weak.

2 The diagrams show the magnetic field lines between two magnets.

Write the letters N or S in each diagram to show the poles of the magnets.

a

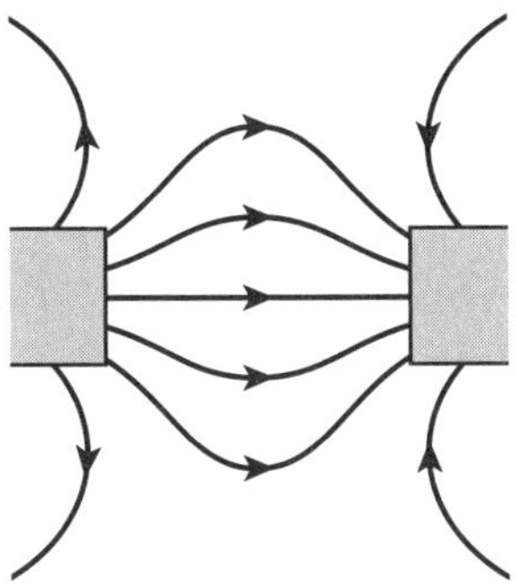

b

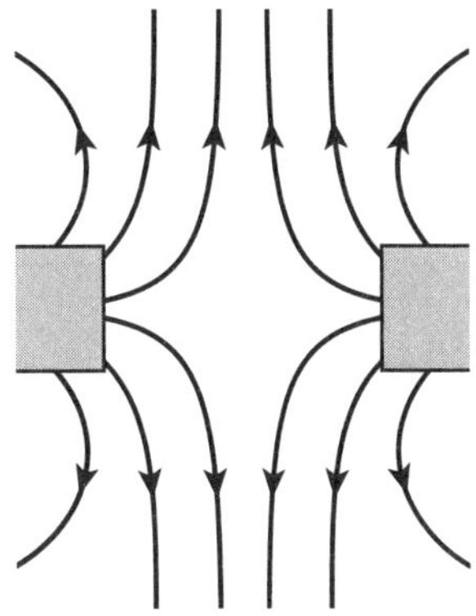

Exercise 9.1B Magnetic fields

Practice

In this exercise, you will describe magnetic fields.

1 a Describe what is meant by the term 'magnetic field'.

....

....

b Describe how you could use a magnetic compass to detect a magnetic field.

....

....

....

2 A bar magnet produces a magnetic field.

Describe how the strength of the magnetic field varies when detected along the directions **a** and **b**.

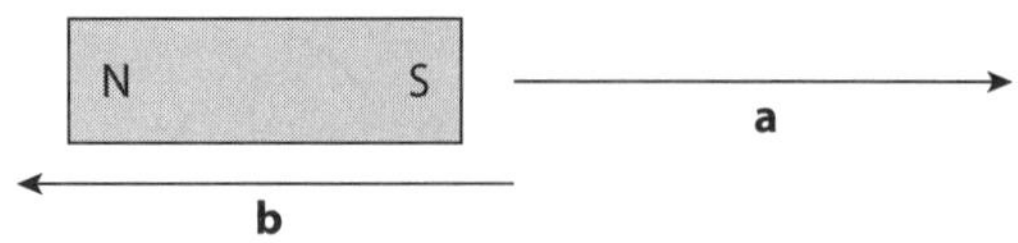

a ....

....

b ....

....

Exercise 9.1C Interaction of magnetic fields

Challenge

In this exercise, you will think about how magnetic fields interact with each other.

1 Two magnetic poles on different magnets are brought together so the magnetic fields interact.

Write the word 'attract' or the word 'repel' after each statement to show the force that will result in each case.

The magnetic field lines between the two poles are in opposite directions. ....

The magnetic field lines between the two poles are in the same direction. ....

2 Describe how a piece of paper and iron filings could be used to show the pattern of the magnetic field between two south poles of different magnets.

....

....

....

....

....

9.2 The Earth as a giant magnet

Exercise 9.2A The Earth's magnetic field

Focus

In this exercise, you will think about the magnetic field around the Earth.

1 Which statements are true about the Earth's magnetic poles?

Tick (✓) all that are correct.

The Earth's magnetic poles have not always been in the same positions. ☐

The Earth's magnetic poles are exactly the same as the geographic poles. ☐

The Earth's magnetic poles are similar to the poles of a bar magnet. ☐

2 Which statement is true about the Earth's magnetic field?

Tick (✓) **one** box.

The Earth's magnetic field occurs only at the poles. ☐

The Earth's magnetic field occurs only at the equator. ☐

The Earth's magnetic field occurs all around the Earth. ☐

The Earth's magnetic field occurs only at certain times. ☐

3 a State the part of the Earth that the Earth's magnetic field comes from.

....

b Name the **two** magnetic metals that make up this part of the Earth.

1 ....

2 ....

Exercise 9.2B Direction of the Earth's magnetic field

Practice

In this exercise, you will think about the direction of the Earth's magnetic field.

1 From a point on the equator of the Earth, in which direction do the Earth's magnetic field lines point?

Tick (✓) **one** box.

toward geographic south ☐

toward geographic north ☐

toward geographic east ☐

toward geographic west ☐

2 If the Earth is represented as a bar magnet, state which magnetic pole of the bar magnet would be closer to geographic north.

....

3 a Describe how a steel needle can be magnetised by using a bar magnet.

....

....

....

....

b Describe how the magnetised needle can be used to show that the Earth has a magnetic field. You may draw a labelled diagram to help your answer.

....

....

....

....

....

....

4 Describe how you could show the direction of the Earth's magnetic field by using:

- a bar magnet
- string
- adhesive tape
- a wooden clamp stand.

You may draw a labelled diagram to help your answer.

....

....

....

....

....

....

....

....

Exercise 9.2C Strength of the Earth's magnetic field

Challenge

In this exercise, you will think about the strength of the Earth's magnetic field.

1 Which of these is stronger?

Tick (✓) **one** box.

the Earth's magnetic field where you live ☐

the strength of the magnetic field 1 cm from the end of a bar magnet ☐

Explain **one** piece of evidence for your choice.

....

....

....

2 The map shows how the strength of the Earth's magnetic field varies in different parts of the world.

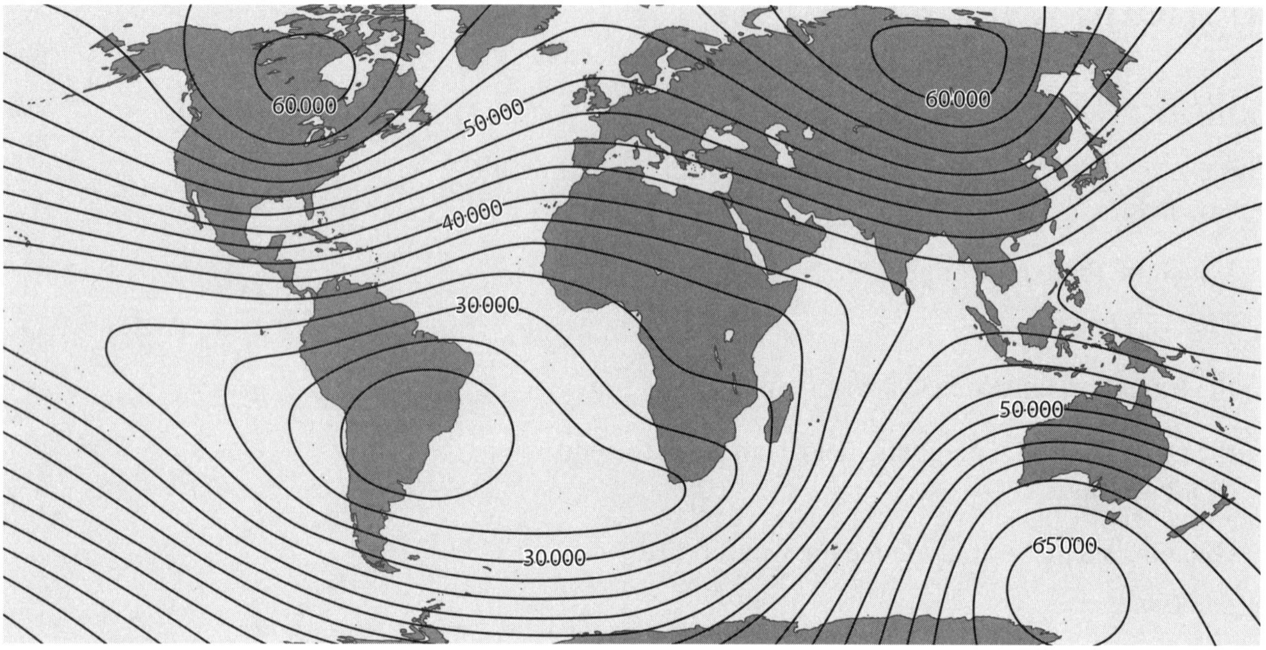

The lines on the map join places where the magnetic field strength is equal.

Some of the lines are labelled with units at intervals of every 10 000 units.

a State the number of lines that must be crossed for the magnetic field strength to increase by 10 000 units.

....

b By how many units does the magnetic field strength change from one of these lines to the next?

....

c On the map, mark with the letter X where the magnetic field is greater than 65 000 units.

d On the map, mark with the letter W where the magnetic field is weakest.

e Write down the magnetic field strength where you live.

.... units

9.3 Electromagnets

Exercise 9.3A Electromagnets 1

Focus

In this exercise, you will think about making an electromagnet.

1 Elsa has:

- a 1.5 V cell
- connectors for use in a circuit
- a switch.

a Write down **two** more things that Elsa needs to make an electromagnet.

1 ....

2 ....

b Which of these could Elsa use to test her electromagnet? Underline **one** thing.

steel paperclips **wooden matchsticks**
grains of salt **pieces of paper**

2 A coil of wire is wrapped around a metal core.

Current is passed through the wire.

Which of these metals could be magnetised when used in the core?

Tick (✓) **two** boxes.

copper ☐

aluminium ☐

steel ☐

gold ☐

iron ☐

3 State **one** way in which an electromagnet is different from a permanent magnet.

....

....

Exercise 9.3B Electromagnets 2

Practice

In this exercise, you will think about how electromagnets work.

1 List **two** applications of electromagnets.

1 ....

2 ....

2 Marcus makes an electromagnet. The electromagnet is shown in the diagram.

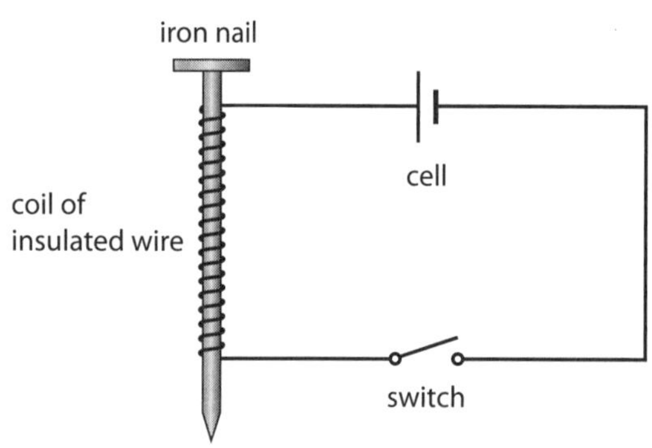

a When the switch is closed, the end of the nail can be used to pick up pins.

Explain why.

....

....

b When the switch is opened, the pins fall off the iron nail.

Explain why.

....

....

c Describe how Marcus could test whether the pointed end of the nail behaves as a north pole or as a south pole.

....

....

....

....

Exercise 9.3C Electromagnets 3

Challenge

In this exercise, you will think in more detail about electromagnets.

1 Zara makes an electromagnet, as shown in the diagram.

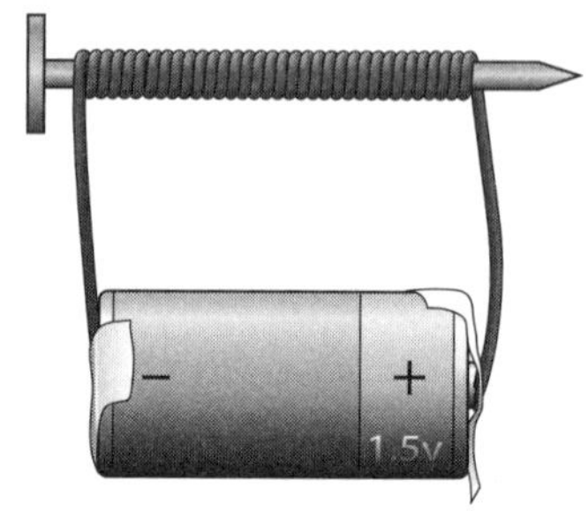

Zara uses the pointed end of the nail to attract paperclips. Zara then writes this hypothesis:

The pointed end of the nail must be the north pole of this electromagnet.

a Explain why this hypothesis could be false.

....

....

b Describe how Zara could use a bar magnet to test her hypothesis.

Include any observations she would make.

....

....

....

....

....

c Zara discovers that the pointed end of the nail is the north pole of this electromagnet.

Suggest **two** changes to this electromagnet that would make the pointed end of the nail become the south pole.

1 ....

....

2 ....

....

9.4 Investigating electromagnets

Exercise 9.4A Strength of electromagnets 1

Focus

In this exercise, you think about the number of turns in the coil and the strength of electromagnets.

1 Marcus investigates how the number of turns on the coil of an electromagnet affects the number of paperclips that the electromagnet can hold.

The table shows his results.

Number of turns on the coil	Number of paperclips lifted
5	1
10	2
15	4
20	5
25	10
30	12
35	16

a Complete the sentences about these results.

As the number of turns on the coil increases, the number of

paperclips lifted ....

This means the electromagnet gets .... as the number of turns on the coil increases.

b Marcus thinks one of his results is anomalous.

Which one?

....

c Suggest what Marcus should do about this anomalous result.

....

....

d Which of these should Marcus keep constant during his investigation.

Tick (✓) all that are correct.

size of the paperclips ☐

current in the coil ☐

number of turns in the coil ☐

material in the core ☐

temperature of the paperclips ☐

type of switch in the circuit ☐

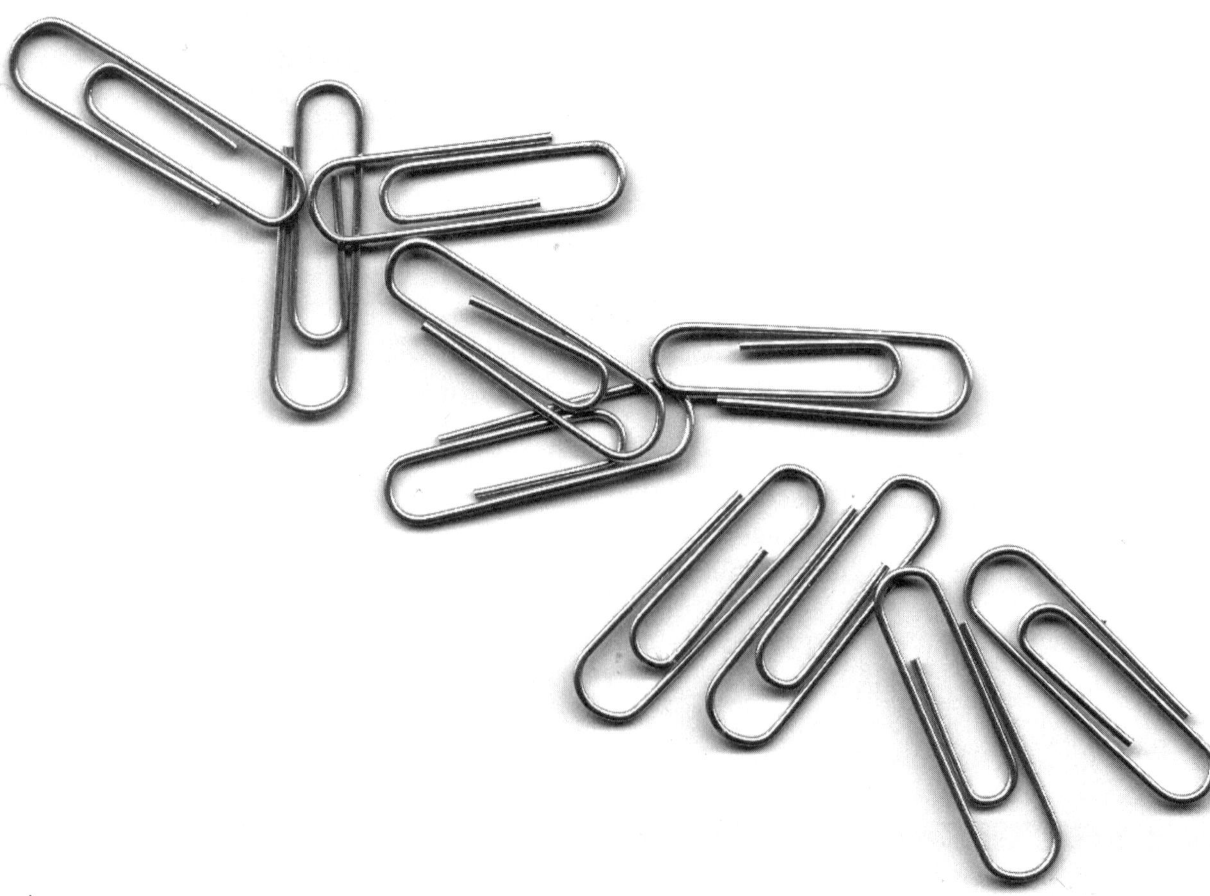

Exercise 9.4B Strength of electromagnets 2

Practice

In this exercise, you think about current in the coil and the strength of electromagnets.

1 Sofia investigates how the current in the coil of an electromagnet affects the strength of the electromagnet.

Sofia measures the strength of the electromagnet by the number of steel pins that can be lifted. All the pins have the same mass.

a List **two** factors that Sofia needs to keep constant in her investigation.

1 ....

2 ....

b Sofia uses an adjustable power supply, like the one shown in the picture.

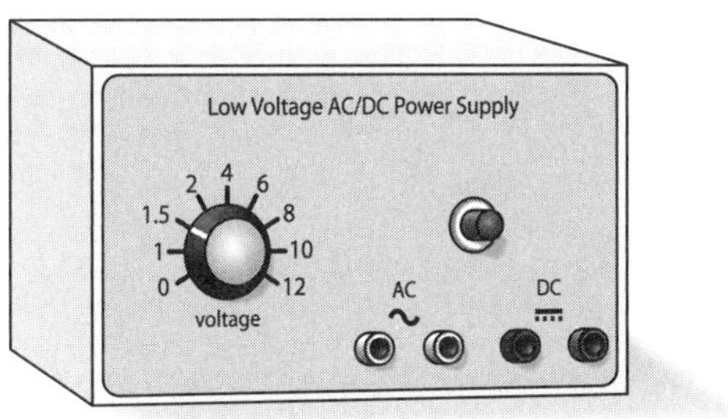

i Describe **two** advantages of using this power supply, in this investigation, compared to changing the number of cells in the circuit.

1 ....

....

2 ....

....

ii What **safety** risk must Sofia be aware of when the current gets larger?

Tick (✓) **one** box.

The electromagnet lifts too many pins. ☐

The wire in the coil gets too hot. ☐

The electromagnet stops working. ☐

The pins get too hot. ☐

c When the current in the circuit is 1.0A, the electromagnet lifts 25 pins.

Suggest the number of pins lifted when the current is:

i 2.0 A

....

ii 0.5 A

....

Exercise 9.4C Strength of electromagnets 3

Challenge

In this exercise, you will think in more detail about measuring the strength of electromagnets.

1 Arun investigates how the number of turns in the coil affects the strength of an electromagnet.

a List **two other** factors that affect the strength of an electromagnet.

1 ....

2 ....

b Arun measures the strength of the electromagnet by finding how many paperclips the electromagnet can hold.

Arun can use large paperclips or small paperclips.

Explain which would give better results.

....

....

....

2 Marcus makes an electromagnet. He arranges the core of the electromagnet vertically above an iron block. The iron block rests on a digital balance. This equipment is shown in the diagram.

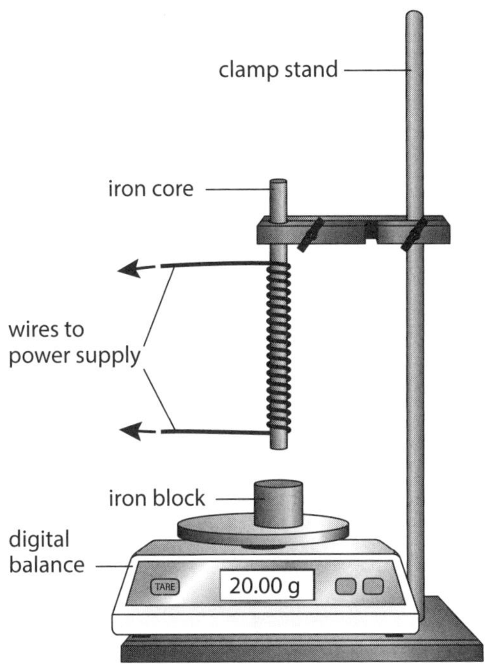

a Explain what will happen to the reading on the digital balance when the electromagnet is switched on.

....

....

....

b Complete this sentence.

As the current in the electromagnet increases, the reading on the balance will ....

c Marcus says 'If the connection from the electromagnet to the power supply is reversed, then the change in readings on the balance will also be reversed.'

Explain whether or not Marcus is correct.

....

....

....

....

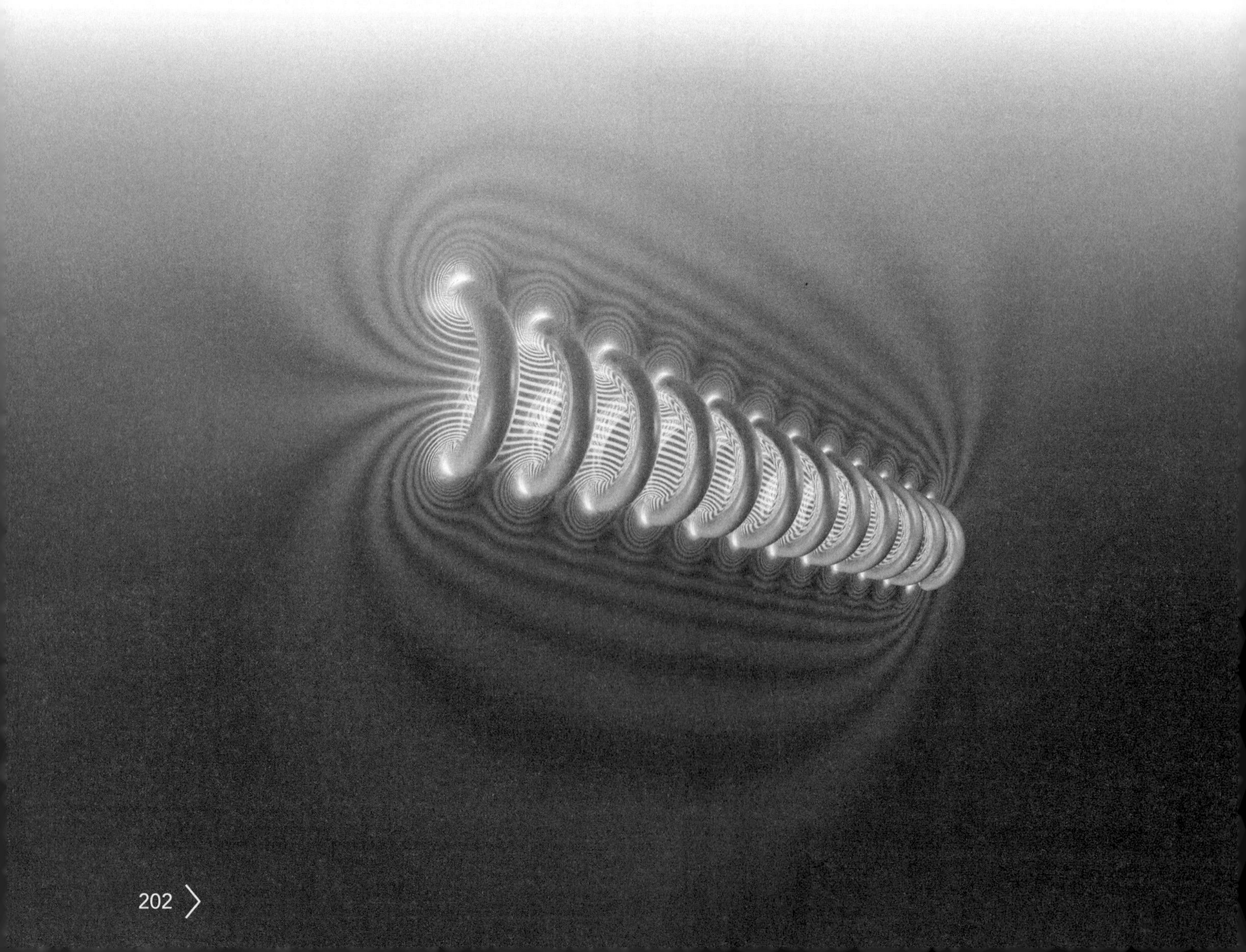